TURN
ME
ON

TURN ME ON

100 EASY WAYS TO USE SOLAR ENERGY

Michelle Kodis

GIBBS SMITH
TO ENRICH AND INSPIRE HUMANKIND
Salt Lake City | Charleston | Santa Fe | Santa Barbara

First Edition
13 12 11 10 09   10 9 8 7 6 5 4 3 2 1

Text © 2009 Michelle Kodis

Published by
Gibbs Smith
P.O. Box 667
Layton, Utah 84041

1.800.835.4993 orders
www.gibbs-smith.com

Designed and produced by Linda Herman, Glyph Publishing Arts
Printed and bound in Canada
Gibbs Smith books are printed on either recycled, 100% post-consumer
waste, FSC-certified papers or on paper produced from a 100% certified
sustainable forest/controlled wood source.

Library of Congress Cataloging-in-Publication Data

Kodis, Michelle.
  Turn me on : 100 easy ways to use solar energy / Michelle Kodis. — 1st ed.
     p. cm.
  ISBN-13: 978-1-4236-0519-5
  ISBN-10: 1-4236-0519-5
  1. Solar energy. I. Title.
  TJ810.K58 2009
  621.47—dc22
                                    2009000068

For Rich, the sunshine of my life

ACKNOWLEDGMENTS

My deepest appreciation and gratitude to: Suzanne Taylor, Michelle Witte, Gibbs Smith, Christopher Robbins, Hollie Keith, Madge Baird, Bob and Joan Kodis, Rosemerry, Kendall, Anne, Maureen, Kierstin, Pam, Marcia, Andrew, Brett, Violet, and Renzo.

CONTENTS

INTRODUCTION

Each month, those of us who live "on the grid" get a little gift in the mail: an invoice for our electricity usage. Prior to that bill arriving, the little meter attached to our homes has been spinning day and night, tallying our energy use as we power up our computers, stuff our wet towels into the dryer, forget to turn off the lights when we leave a room, pop in a DVD, fire up the coffee-maker, and so on. Our debt to the power company can fluctuate depending on the season. In winter, of course, we can't do without that toasty electric blanket, right? When indeed the bill is higher in the winter months, we sigh, thinking that we really should start finding ways to reduce our fossil fuel consumption and do our part for the planet—but it all seems so . . . complex and time-consuming, and we don't know where to start. We write the check and it's on to next month. *Click. Click. Click.* That's the sound of the meter costing you money. Ready to learn about a new way? Read on.

Currently, the United States is a fossil fuel–dependent nation. We could not function without the grid, the intricate and vast network of electrical utility distribution. When you hear about a person who lives "off the grid," this means he or she has either fully or partially ended dependence on the grid for energy by substituting alternative means of generating power. While *Turn Me On* does not aim to get you grid-independent by early next week, we do hope it will provide the inspiration and impetus to learn more about the ways—some of them very, very easy and very, very free—to end total reliance on diminishing fossil fuels.

I wholeheartedly thank and salute you for choosing this book. In doing so, you have joined an unstoppable global movement that is transforming, at seemingly warp speed, how we view the inherent limitations of our precious natural resources. That movement is giving us intelligent and innovative new choices for how we conduct our lives. Maybe you already know a thing or two about solar power, or perhaps you've chosen this book to begin building a knowledge base to get you started on a more in-depth path toward renewable energy. Whatever your individual experience or goal, I hope *Turn Me On* helps you develop a passion for solar power that you will pass on to others.

As the third title in Gibbs Smith's series of "eco" handbooks (the first two, *It's Easy Being Green* and *Go Green,* have enjoyed much-deserved success), *Turn Me On* is a lively and educational glimpse at all things solar. In these pages, you'll find everything from descriptions about the latest and greatest technology to how to use a simple solar oven. From the outset, my goal in compiling this body of information was to give you as many ideas and tidbits for thought as possible without overwhelming you with too much technical detail and data. My guess is that after reading *Turn Me On* you'll be craving a deeper understanding of both technology and policy, and you'll find plenty of additional reading suggestions in these pages.

Turn Me On does not have a fancy table of contents or clever organizational tactics. It is a straightforward, sequential, 1 to 100 journey of ideas, insights, technology, science, collaboration, inspiration, surprises, guidance, and, even, pop culture. And, it has been designed to guide you through the information as effortlessly as possible; for that I am indebted to the talented graphic designer, Linda Herman, who took my words and shaped them into a cohesive book that I hope will have a positive influence on your life, and on the lives of those around you.

The snappy title, courtesy of Gibbs Smith vice president and editorial director, Suzanne Taylor, and the cheerful art on the cover and throughout the text, clearly indicate that we are having some fun with this topic. We're not going to go into any heavy detail. We promise you we won't get pedantic or pushy. This handbook is a springboard. Use it, share it, add to it using the blank journal pages at the end of the book. Here's the deal, folks: environmentalism does not have to be a heart-heavy endeavor in which the constant reminder of a planet in peril permeates our collective daily mood. Quite the opposite. There is great hope to be had as this book enters the marketplace. Across the world, great thinkers, innovators, and leaders are searching for and discovering ways to shift to clean, renewable energy. Every day, it seems, a new development or trend in sustainability and alternative energy arrives, reminding us to always look on the bright side of things.

—*Michelle Kodis*

1

SHOULD YOU CARE ABOUT CARBON?

The following essay, "Why Carbon Matters," is courtesy of Carbon Monitoring for Action (CARMA), **www.carma.org.** Through its massive database of information on the carbon emissions of more than 50,000 power plants and 4,000 power companies worldwide, CARMA aims to equip individuals with the information they need to forge a cleaner, low-carbon future. CARMA is produced and financed by the Confronting Climate Change Initiative at the Center for Global Development, an independent and non-partisan think tank located in Washington, D.C. This essay is an excellent explanation of why renewable energy sources are more crucial than ever to the sustained health of the planet. (This essay is reprinted with permission from the Center for Global Development, **www.cgdev.org** / **www.carma.org.**)

The bulk of humanity's energy needs are currently met through the combustion of fossil fuels like coal, oil, and natural gas. About 60 percent of global electricity generation relies upon fossil fuels to make the heat needed to power steam-driven turbines. Burning these fuels results in the production of carbon dioxide (CO_2)—the primary heat-trapping "greenhouse gas" responsible for global warming.

If our greenhouse gas emissions succeed in pushing the climate past the point of no return, we are unlikely to realize it until it is too late to avoid the consequences.

Over the past two centuries, mankind has increased the concentration of CO_2 in the atmosphere from 280 to more than 380 parts per million volume, and it is growing faster every day. The atmospheric concentration of CO_2 has not been this high for at least the past 650,000 years. As the concentration of CO_2

has risen, so has the average temperature of the planet. Over the past century, the average surface temperature of Earth has increased by more than 1.3°F (0.74°C). If we continue to emit carbon without restraint, temperatures are expected to rise by an additional 6°F (3.4°C) by the end of this century.

Climate change of that magnitude would likely have serious consequences for life on Earth. Sea level rise, droughts, floods, intense storms, forest fires, water scarcity, and cardio-respiratory and tropical diseases would be exacerbated. Agricultural systems would be stressed—possibly decimated in some parts of the world. A conservative estimate suggests that 30 percent of all species are at risk of extinction given current trends. It would be the greatest extinction of life on Earth since the K-T extinction event that destroyed the dinosaurs 65 million years ago. No one can imagine—never mind predict—the ecological consequences of such a radical loss of life.

Mankind probably needs to reduce total CO_2 emissions by at least 80 percent by 2050.

There is also the risk that continued warming will push the planet past critical thresholds or "tipping points"—like the large-scale melting of polar ice, the thawing of tundra or methane clathrates, the collapse of the Amazon rain forest, or the warming and acidification of the oceans—that will make further climate change inescapable and irreversible. The history of Earth suggests that such positive feedback loops in the climate system are powerful and often severe. If our greenhouse gas emissions succeed in pushing the climate past the point of no return, we are unlikely to realize it until it is too late to avoid the consequences.

Despite mounting evidence of the dangers posed by climate change, efforts to limit carbon emissions remain insufficient, ineffective, and, in most countries, non-existent. If the world is to avert the worst consequences of an altered climate, the status quo must change quickly. Given current trends and the best available scientific evidence, mankind probably needs to reduce total CO_2 emissions by at least 80 percent by 2050. Yet each day emissions continue to grow.

In the absence of action on the part of governments, hundreds of millions of increasingly climate-conscious citizens can promote low-carbon alternatives by changing the ways they purchase, invest, vote, think, and live. All you need to act is timely, accurate, publicly available information about the choices you face. It's time to take matters into your own hands.

In the absence of action on the part of governments, hundreds of millions of increasingly climate-conscious citizens can promote low-carbon alternatives by changing the ways they purchase, invest, vote, think, and live.

2

THIS AIN'T YOUR GRANDMA'S SOLAR

In one corner, we have the Sun. In the other corner, the collective "us," otherwise known as the people of the world. We need electricity for myriad reasons. The Sun can provide that energy. What, then, is the formula?

In its essence, the sunshine-to-electricity conversion is not complicated. You have solar radiance (sunlight). That sunlight is collected by silicon photovoltaic (PV) cells. As sunlight hits the cells, electrons are set free, producing electricity. A group of PV cells is called a PV module. The module produces direct current (DC), again, via those free-wheeling electrons. But, DC likely won't work in your home. Why? Because your home is set up for alternating current (AC). This is where the inverter comes in: its job is to convert DC to AC. If you don't need the electricity right away, you can store it in a battery, for later use or on overcast days when the module is not performing at its optimal level. The battery also gives a grid-tied home a backup in the event of a power outage. In addition, charge controllers are necessary for regulating voltage and current moving from the PV module to the battery, preventing damage to the battery from overcharging.

Think of it this way: **PV modules** (harness the energy of sunlight)→**Charge controller** (regulates voltage, prevents battery from overcharging)→**Battery** (stores electricity for later use)→**Inverter** (converts DC to AC)→**End Result:** electricity flowing into the home.

ACTIVELY SOLAR

Active solar is exactly what it sounds like: an actively working solar cell or panel array that uses a series of controls and pumps designed to harness the sun's energy to power your home and heat water.

QUICK TIP

- Protect your PV array's storage battery from over-charging with a charge controller, also called a regulator. The charge controller controls the flow of current to and from the battery and can also monitor overall system performance.

4

SOLAR QUERIES

Here are answers to a few questions you might have about solar.

Why is solar power getting so much attention lately?
It's all about the word "renewable." Unlike power generated by
limited and quickly depleting natural resources (fossil fuels), solar
energy is boundless. The sun produces clean energy without creating the pollutants that contribute to climate change.

**But wait—doesn't the manufacturing of photovoltaics cause
pollution, too?**
Yes, the production of PV cells does create emissions, but studies
show that solar produces less than 15 percent of the carbon
dioxide from a traditional coal-fired power plant. According to
the Environmental Protection Agency, a million homes converted to
solar would reduce carbon dioxide emissions by 4.3 million tons
per year, which is roughly equal to taking 850,000 cars off the road.

Do I need a certain type of house in order to convert to solar?
No, not necessarily. A broad south-facing roof would nicely
accommodate solar panels—if your neighborhood design rules
permit this (make sure you contact your local building department before you embark on a solar retrofit). Photovoltaic panels
can be installed as freestanding arrays if the configuration of
your house doesn't work for solar. New homes have the advantage in that solar rooftop materials can be built directly into the
structure. The reality is this: solar technology is advancing
rapidly, which is good news for consumers because the ways
in which solar can be installed are expanding.

Will I really see savings in my utility bills?
In a word, yes. Solar energy systems can significantly lower your
monthly utility bill. Here's something else you may not have

considered: PV panels will shade your roof by bouncing back all that heat that otherwise would be absorbed and thus increase indoor air temperatures. When you keep your rooms at a nice, cool temperature in the summer, the need for air-conditioning is greatly reduced.

Should I expect to replace my solar array often? I can't afford to do that!

No! The beauty of PV technology is that the panels are designed to last a very long time, depending on levels of active use (most systems are in use for no more than eight hours per day, more likely less) and how much sunshine is being converted into electricity by the individual cells. Most manufacturers provide long-term warranties of 10–20 years, but a solar installer will tell you that the panels will probably outlive the warranty.

Will I have to spend every weekend maintaining my PV array?

Again, no. Because it has no moving parts, a PV system is straightforward and pretty much maintenance-free. If you have a grid-connected array, you will be required to keep the panels clean and clear of debris.

SOLAR GIZMOS

- Interested in an outdoor shower? For about $20, you can purchase a Super Solar Shower. Place it in direct sun on a 70-degree day and it will heat five gallons of water from 60 degrees to 108 degrees.

- Wilting under the hot sun? Need a soothing breeze to cool you off? The Solar Hat Fan is ready for rescue. The small fan is designed to clamp onto a hat, and it begins to spin as the unit's tiny photovoltaic panel soaks up the sun's rays. At only $10 each, consider buying a bunch to give as gifts.

5

SOAK UP THOSE RAYS

It sounds, well, a bit of a snooze-fest, but passive solar energy can be put to good active use. Radiant heat from the sun can be manipulated and controlled to heat and cool interiors, in the process reducing energy consumption and resulting in an energy-efficient dwelling and less money spent on the power company.

The three approaches to a passive setup are **direct gain** (interiors soak up and store sunlight, release heat at night), **indirect gain** (thermal storage wall systems, roof ponds), and **isolate gain** (sunroom, convective loop through air collector, then heat is stored in-house). Your mission? To capture that precious solar warmth within the building and then release it when the sun is behind clouds or at night.

A few basic things to consider:

1. To ensure the most successful passive solar design, choose a site with plenty of solar exposure. Sound obvious? Perhaps, but this main point can sometimes be forgotten in the heady excitement of design and construction. Avoid wooded lots, and be aware of any trees whose growth may eventually impede your home's passive solar capabilities.

2. Orient and lengthen the building along an east–west axis. This ensures plenty of solar-friendly southern exposure. Also, make sure that southern exposure provides at least six hours of powerful sunlight during the cooler months.

3. For solar heating, place the bulk of the glazing on the south-facing facade.

4. Overhangs are crucial to helping control the temperature inside the house. Solar experts in the *Real Goods Solar Living Source Book* explain, "Overhangs on the south side are the on-off switches of a passive solar house." Unless you want to roast in your living room, don't forget the overhangs.

5. You'll find many online sources of information about passive solar. I was helped in my efforts with "A Sourcebook for Green and Sustainable Building," published by the fantastic **www.greenbuilder.com,** a website you should bookmark and get to know in detail. Also, the *Real Goods* solar book described earlier includes a detailed section on the topic, as does *The Complete Idiot's Guide to Solar Power for Your Home*. Both sources include illustrations that nicely demonstrate the concepts at hand.

6. According to the *Idiot's* book, a sunroom is an excellent investment in eco-living and quality of life. Authors Ramsey and Hughes point out: "A well-designed sunspace can provide up to 60 percent of a home's winter heating requirements. In addition, it can offer overnight warmth, summer cooling, and a great place to stretch out and read a book by natural light." Well said!

GET PV'D

Photovoltaics (PV) convert sunlight into electricity. How does this work, exactly? The naturally occurring photons in sunlight represent energy. A solar cell or panel absorbs these photons, at which point a crucial meeting of the minds occurs: the photons interact with the electrons stored in the PV material, exciting and agitating the electrons until the electrons break free to form a current. These free-wheeling electrons need a place to go, so they are directed to batteries for storage for later use, or directed into the building that houses the PV panels for immediate use in powering appliances and other items that require electricity.

WHAT'S YOUR TYPE?

Solar cells, also called PV cells, are small, semi-conducting elements designed to convert sunlight into a "direct current" form of electrical energy. Solar cells wired together form a PV module. The size of a PV module is determined by available sunlight and how much electricity is needed, on a case-by-case basis. The basic types of solar cells are:

Monocrystalline/Single Crystal Silicon: The most widely used. Also tend to be more expensive than other kinds.

Polycrystalline: Less costly than single-crystal silicon cells but not the most efficient when it comes to converting energy.

Amorphous: Widely available and relatively less expensive to produce. They are "without" shape, which means that their silicon is not crystallized or highly structured.

8

ENLIGHTEN ME

Solar panels can be used to:
1. Convert sunlight into electricity via solar cells set on PV modules.
2. Heat water, oil, or antifreeze via solar thermal collectors.

When choosing your solar panels, keep the following in mind:

Cost: How many do you need? How durable are they? Will they need to be replaced soon? Factor maintenance into general cost calculations.

Type: If you want to go solar on a camping trip, you likely won't need the same type of solar panel as you would for residential use. Research solar panels by use; in other words, which are best suited to the task at hand?

Size: Maximum wattage is determined by the size of the panel, as well as the type of solar cells used for the panel. The larger the panel, the more electrical output it has.

Longevity: A good solar installer will direct you toward the options that best fit your needs and budget. Different types of solar cells have different life spans, so pick the one with the longest life span that you can afford. How the panels are framed can make a big difference, too. For example, lightweight and durable aluminum is a popular framing material for solar arrays.

FORM AN ATTACHMENT

Solar panels can be attached to your home or arranged in a "free-standing" configuration set apart from the building. Where you ultimately decide to place your PV array will depend on a number of factors, including:

* your neighborhood and its particular set of design rules, which likely will dictate how solar panels can be presented on a building;
* local topography and the immediate landscape around your home. For example, if your home is surrounded by tall trees that block sunlight, you would be advised to place your PV array in a sunny location away from the house;
* building restrictions, such as an architectural design that precludes the placement of roof-mount solar panels on the house;
* personal taste: maybe you love the idea of using the sun to power your home, but you don't necessarily want to see PV panels as you drive up to the front door (there are other solutions to this challenge, such as solar shingles and other new technologies, discussed later in the book).

Your solar installer will make the best recommendation based on your needs and, of course, budget.

EMPOWERED CO-DEPENDENCY

If you're not yet ready to exert your energy independence by going "off the grid," then a grid-tied solar power system could be the right choice. Grid-tied systems essentially act as adjunct power supplies; they augment the electricity coming into your home from the local power company.

Grid-tied folks can enjoy the financial benefits of net metering, a government incentive program that encourages the use of renewables by allowing individual and business consumers who generate excess electricity via non–fossil fuel sources such as solar and wind to "sell" that power back to the local utility in the form of a retail credit. Although net metering rules tend to vary by state, the Energy Policy Act of 2005 mandated that all public electric utilities offer net metering to their customers.

Homeowners feel pride in their eco-friendly contribution. In their experience of creating and using renewable power, they are *empowered*.

So, on sunny days, when a single household does not require all of the power it's generating via its PV panels, the owner of that household can sell this excess electricity back to his power company. On cloudy days, and at night, the household will use power from the grid. The end result is that the consumer's utility costs are calculated on his net electricity usage.

The thrill goes beyond saving money, though. Homeowners who partake in such programs speak of feeling more aware of their overall energy use, and on average they tend to use less energy, thanks to this heightened knowledge. They feel pride in their eco-friendly contribution. In their experience of creating and using renewable power, they are empowered.

The downside? Let's say the grid is down due to inclement weather. That means you are without electricity. Unless you . . .

11
ALWAYS HAVE A BACKUP

Essentially a more sophisticated (and more expensive) version of the basic grid-tied PV system, the grid-tied battery backup option protects you if the grid is down. How? It's actually quite simple: the inverter that converts direct current (DC) to usable alternating current (AC) is connected to a battery, which is charged by the solar panels. If grid-fed power suddenly stops, the inverter automatically disconnects from the grid and begins to draw power from the charged battery. Voilà! You have backup power!

GOING ALL THE WAY

Okay. You've taken the time to educate yourself about renewable energy generated by solar panels. You have taken a deep
breath (or two, perhaps three). You are ready to sever all ties to
the utility company. You are going *off-grid*.

Off-grid is exactly that: any power coming into your home to
power appliances is generated solely by your solar panel array.
A backup generator is recommended in case of emergency and
to make up for power lost to overcast days.

YES YOU CAN

- If you feel you can't afford to install a solar package in your home, think again: many solar vendors
  offer financing to help pay for your new system.
  Take the time to shop for the products with the
  best interest rates.

13

DELIVERING POWER

You're probably already familiar with this technology: the ability to run your computer when a lightning strike takes out the grid, for example. An uninterruptible power supply (UPS) employs a battery to provide extra run time for appliances in the event of a power outage. Consider a UPS if you can't afford downtime (for example, you work at home) or if you use electricity-powered medical equipment.

INVERT ME, BABY

Without an inverter, the electrical energy collected by your PV system will remain in an unusable form. Inverters convert low-voltage direct current power (DC), which originates at the array or is stored in the battery, to high-voltage alternating current (AC), the electrical power accessible through any standard wall socket. The DC-to-AC conversion automatically results in a loss of power, but this can be mitigated by taking time to find an inverter with a rated efficiency score of 90 percent or more.

Also crucial: ensuring that your inverter's output power matches the maximum wattage capacity of your solar panel or array.

A full discussion of solar inverters is beyond the scope of this book, but you can find plenty of information online and from solar suppliers. Don't be hesitant to ask solar installers which inverters they prefer, and inquire about customer testimonials.

CHARGE IT!

If you want to hang on to all that delicious DC electricity your solar panels are soaking up, you will need a battery. Lead-acid deep cycle batteries, the most commonly used in PV arrays, are designed specially to handle the vagaries of the weather—for example, one day with full sunshine followed by a day with overcast skies and the subsequent charging and discharging that occurs as energy needs wax and wane.

Although lead-acid batteries are more expensive than conventional batteries (such as those used in cars) they do boast a longer shelf life. The key to an optimally performing solar array is a battery ideally matched to the system. In other words, if you choose a battery that is too small to accommodate your system, it will likely discharge too often and require sooner-than-normal replacement. Expect your lead-acid battery to last a good dozen years, if cared for properly.

Battery capacity is measured in ampere-hours (Ah). Individual battery cells contained in the unit store electrical energy channeled in from solar panels. For maximum storage of power, your solar installer might recommend a battery bank: several batteries wired together. The benefits of a battery bank are clear: collected energy is stored for use on overcast days and at night, and should your household require more power than your array is producing at any given moment, the battery backup can be called upon to meet higher energy needs.

You can extend the life of your battery by doing the following: (Thanks to **www.solarguide.com** for this battery-saving to-do list)

- Fully charge the battery before use.
- Tighten the connectors.
- Tightly fasten the vent caps.
- Check the battery regularly for signs of corrosion, and, if present, remove the corrosion, as well as any accumulated dirt and dust.
- Water the battery after extended charging and check the acid level after charging.
- Avoid filling or overfilling the cells: as the battery charges, electrolyte matter can overflow, resulting in corrosion and shortening the life of the battery.
- Use distilled water.

TAKE CHARGE

Without a charge controller, you might as well kiss your battery good-bye—and plan to spend your hard-earned cash replacing it with a new one, and then another one, and . . . well, you get the picture.

The charge controller's job is to protect the battery from taking in too much charge and losing too much charge. An out-of-control battery that overcharges and over-discharges is a battery not long for this world. The charge controller, which is placed between the solar panel(s) and the battery/battery bank, ensures a consistent and maximum charge. This even-keeled state of existence will also extend the life of the battery.

17

ENVIRONMENTAL STEWARD: BARACK OBAMA

"We will harness the sun and the winds and the soil to fuel our cars and run our factories . . ."

—President Barack Obama, inaugural speech, January 20, 2009

The election of Barack Obama as the 44th president of the United States sent up a collective cheer of hope and relief from environmentalists around the world. President Obama has pledged to focus on issues of renewable energy and conservation, and the timing could not be better.

Here are a few highlights from the comprehensive Obama/Biden energy plan:

* Provide short-term relief to American families facing pain at the pump.
* Help create 5 million new jobs by strategically investing $150 billion over the next 10 years to catalyze private efforts to build a clean energy future.
* Within 10 years save more oil than is currently imported from the Middle East and Venezuela combined.

- Put 1 million plug-in hybrid cars—which can get up to 150 miles per gallon—on the road by 2015, cars that they will work to make sure are built in America.
- Ensure 10 percent of electricity comes from renewable sources by 2012, and 25 percent by 2025.
- Implement an economy-wide cap-and-trade program to reduce greenhouse gas emissions 80 percent by 2050.
- Enact a Windfall Profits Tax to provide a $1,000 Emergency Energy Rebate to American families.
- Crack down on excessive energy speculation.
- Swap oil from the Strategic Petroleum Reserve to cut prices.
- Eliminate current imports from the Middle East and Venezuela within 10 years.
- Increase fuel economy standards.
- Create a new $7,000 tax credit for purchasing advanced vehicles.
- Establish a national low-carbon-fuel standard.
- A "Use It or Lose It" approach to existing oil and gas leases.
- Promote the responsible domestic production of oil and natural gas.
- Weatherize 1 million homes annually.
- Develop and deploy clean coal technology.

18 THE COLD HARD FACTS ABOUT COAL

Big Coal: The Dirty Secret Behind America's Energy Future should be mandatory reading. Its warnings about the dire consequences of a national reliance on coal reads like a horror-flick marquee: "Each American uses approximately 20 pounds of coal each day to fuel our power-hungry life"; "Coal-fired power plants account for 40 percent of the carbon dioxide emissions into the atmosphere"; and "In just the past 20 years, air pollution from coal plants has killed more than half a million Americans." You get the picture. In his groundbreaking book, Goodell makes it clear what will happen if we don't get a handle on our coal-devouring ways. Get a copy. Read it. Be forever changed.

GROWTH SPURTS

The market research firm NanoMarkets projects significant revenue growth for thin-film photovoltaics manufacturers in the coming years. Studies on PV markets reveal an enormous anticipated increase, from the $2.4 billion in estimated 2008 revenues to more than $12 billion in 2013. In addition, the market is set to double by 2015, to some $22 billion.

SIZZLING SOLAR JOBS

Industrial Machinery Mechanic
9 percent projected growth
$42,350 median annual income

Someone has to install solar panels and repair wind turbines, and industrial machinery mechanics are often the ones who get the jobs. In solar, Tioga Energy's executive vice president Preston Roper said the biggest demand is for solar installers.

Local community colleges are the places to get training necessary for the jobs. Many are offering specialized training in solar or wind repair work.

GET YOUR COMPONENTS IN ORDER

If you're ready to purchase a solar power system for your home, the process will inevitably be easier to navigate if you choose a pre-designed solar package or hire a specialized supplier or contractor.

As Dan Ramsey points out in his brilliant book, *The Complete Idiot's Guide to Solar Power for your Home*, "There's no such thing as a typical photovoltaic system, which is a complete set of components for converting sunlight into electricity by the photovoltaic process, including the array and balance of system components."

Well said, Dan. He goes on to list the common components of any PV system. Smaller systems will not have all the components; the larger ones will. Some of these we've already discussed.

Why not dedicate a special notebook to your solar project? Start it off by listing these solar system components. And, should you want considerably more detail on this subject than this introductory guide offers, definitely invest in Ramsey's excellent book.

SYSTEM COMPONENTS:

* **PV modules**: take sunlight, make electricity.
* **Mounting**: Supports PV modules on a building or on a free-standing array. Orients modules toward sun.
* **Combiner/fusing**: Combines and protects module output wiring.
* **Inverter**: Converts DC to usable AC.
* **Batteries**: Store DC electricity.
* **Charge Controller**: Regulates battery charge and prevents over- and under-charging.
* **Monitor/metering**: Reports system status (current and cumulative) and system flows.
* **Generator**: Provides backup AC power.
* **Power Center**: Encloses controller, overcurrent protection, and monitors in one location.
* **Wiring**: Connects components, allowing flow of electricity.
* **Breakers/Fuses**: Protect against electrical overload.

22
MISS CALCULATION

Each solar array has its own set of particulars, among them budget, location, and individual energy needs. Here are a few useful tips for determining the size of your PV system:

Your geographic location: some locales are sunnier than others. Areas with high numbers of sunny days per year will give you more bang for your solar buck. Maps and charts are available to help you determine average hours of full sun per day, per season.

Professional solar installers use solar calculators to determine energy needs. However, it's unreasonable to expect to calculate a single, set-in-stone number. Be willing to be flexible, and take into consideration the following: Do you want a solar system to provide the bulk of your energy needs, or a partial sum? Is the PV array for a weekend house, versus a full-time dwelling? How do your energy usage trends vary from season to season? Do you use your appliances more frequently during certain parts of the day or week?

Your energy needs will be described in watt hours, watts, or kilowatt hours (KWh). While a medium-sized PV panel might provide an average of 50 watts, a larger panel can bring you above 200 watts.

A variety of solar calculators can be found online, including at the following websites:

www.findsolar.com
www.pvwatts.org
http://solar.sharpusa.com
www.thesolarguide.com

23

RUDOLPH'S NOT SO BRIGHT ANYMORE

No, Santa hasn't gone solar . . . yet. But come Christmastime, you can decorate the exterior of your home the eco-friendly way with strings of solar-powered lights. Sounds simple, but you will want to take the following into consideration before purchasing:

Different products will have differing illumination times. The average illumination period is about 7–8 hours, but daytime weather will ultimately determine how charged your lights are at night, and subsequently how long they stay lit.

The next question: blinking or steady? Some versions offer the best of both worlds via a switch that easily changes the twinkle factor.

Review the lights' battery requirements. Yes, solar-powered lights need a way to store charge—and that's where the battery comes in. Some manufacturers use non-rechargeable lithium batteries in their lights, while others use rechargeable batteries.

You can decorate the exterior of your home the eco-friendly way with strings of solar-powered lights.

Prepare for potential sticker shock: solar holiday lights will likely cost more than their traditional peers, but you'll notice the savings on your post-season utility bills.

Where to find them? If you're Internet savvy, try Googling "solar Christmas lights" and you'll find many vendors. Otherwise, inquire at your local stores for availability.

24
FIND A MAN TO DO YOUR BIDDING

If you're not confident or skilled enough to install your solar power system yourself, it's time to find a PV provider to do the work for you.

This will be an important relationship! Now that you have decided to take the plunge and invest your hard-earned money on renewable energy for your home, you want the process of researching options and installing your chosen system to be as smooth as possible. Finding the right PV provider for you could take some time; be patient and willing to wait until you've struck the right chord, both professionally and personally. Pay attention to your gut feelings—they won't steer you down the wrong path. Your stomach aside, here are some tips to keep in mind:

One of the best ways to find a quality installer is through referrals. Don't be shy about finding out as much as you can about your candidates—you'll save yourself from migraines later on in the process.

This is key: DOES THE INSTALLER HAVE THE TIME TO COMPLETE YOUR PROJECT IN A TIMELY MANNER? Why, you might be asking yourself right now, did I put that last sentence in cautionary CAPS? Because, I tell ya, human nature can be an unbridled Pollyanna. Make sure your interviews with candidates include a discussion about realistic timing. Also, keep yourself in check with your own expectations—are you in a hurry, do you want your solar system installed yesterday? Take a breath,

One of the best ways to find a quality installer is through referrals. Don't be shy about finding out as much as you can about your candidates— you'll save yourself from migraines later on in the process.

shake down those shoulders, and remember that this is a long-term investment of time and money. Be willing to compromise on the timing, but be ultra-careful when confronted with an installer who promises you the moon.

Ask to see your candidate's license, and take note of his license number. What renewable energy certification and/or training does he have under his belt? Does he understand local and national rebate scenarios that might save you money? Also, make sure the candidate has a valid contractor license and ask if he would be willing to post a performance bond (a guarantee that the job will be completed as per the contract) and whether he has an active worker's comp policy. Request an example of the bid process, and insist on clarity when it comes to how the candidate hires subcontractors and how he approaches and works with lenders.

Finally, if you have an attorney, it's wise to ask him to review all contracts before you embark on your solar adventure.

25

SHINING EXAMPLE

As president of Solar Design Associates (SDA), Steven Strong is at the forefront of solar technology and the integration of renewable energy systems. Named an environmental hero by *Time* magazine in 1999 and "Environmental Entrepreneur of the Year" by the Audubon Society in 2003—just two of many prestigious honors and awards—Strong has worked long and hard to advance the cause of moving away from fossil fuels and into a new realm of Earth-friendly energy.

Strong, who founded SDA in 1974, had been working prior to that as an engineering consultant on the Alaskan pipeline. That job convinced him there were "easier, less-costly and more environmentally desirable" ways to deal with the nation's energy needs than "going to the ends of the earth to extract the last drop of fossil fuel."

With his background in architecture and engineering, Strong has earned SDA an international reputation for finding new ways to integrate solar electricity into environmentally responsible design. His list of projects is too long for this book, but here are some highlights:

* Electric Sunflowers: SDA's response to clients who wanted to power their country home and vineyard in the Napa Valley. The clients mandated that the system be efficient, reliable, enjoyable to look at, and fun. Strong's company proposed a large array of electric sunflowers on a steep, south-facing hillside on the client's property. The sunflowers track the sun from dawn to dusk and then return to their starting place to begin the process again the next day. "Tracking enhances the solar harvest while creating what the clients refer to as a 'hillside of kinetic art,'" explains Strong. To see a photo of these magnificent sunflowers, go to **www.solardesign.com** and search under "Projects."

* Solar-Powered Gas Stations: When BP made the environmentally forward decision to use solar to power their gas stations, they hired SDA to design, engineer, and construct the appropriate solar array technology. Existing flat-panel canopies were topped with low-profile crystalline arrays. For new stations, SDA designed a shallow, barrel-vaulted canopy glazed with transparent PV elements.

* Solar-Powered Olympics: Strong's company provided design and engineering support to architects working on the Olympic Village for the 1996 summer games in Atlanta, Georgia. The Olympic Natatorium's main roof features a large PV array and a solar-thermal system to warm the competition pools. SDA also designed the custom arched-glass PV canopy that served as the entry to the Olympic venue.

GO SOLAR!

In August 2008, the U.S. Department of Energy (DOE) announced it would invest up to $24 million in fiscal year 2008 and beyond to develop solar energy products to "significantly accelerate penetration of solar photovoltaic (PV) systems in the United States."

The program aims to make electricity generated by PV systems cost-competitive with conventional grid-tied electricity by 2015. The Solar America Initiative (SAI) has partnered with industry, statewide universities, state governments, federal agencies, and other non-governmental agencies to boost the economy by creating a U.S.-based solar industry, as well as diversifying the nation's electricity portfolio, working to reduce the effects of power outages in major metropolitan areas, and reducing the overall environmental impact of power generation from fossil fuels, nuclear energy, and natural gas.

Also part of the initiative is the Solar America Cities program, which has gathered twenty-five U.S. cities to partner with the DOE to support the goals of SAI. Participating cities have expressed their commitment to accelerating the adoption and integration of solar technology at the local level. The cities are:

Seattle, WA	Milwaukee, WI
Portland, OR	Ann Arbor, MI
Berkeley, CA	Pittsburgh, PA
San Francisco, CA	Philadelphia, PA
Santa Rosa, CA	New York, NY
Sacramento, CA	Boston, MA
San Jose, CA	Austin, TX
San Diego, CA	Houston, TX
Salt Lake City, UT	San Antonio, TX
Denver, CO	New Orleans, LA
Tucson, AZ	Knoxville, TN
Minneapolis/St. Paul, MN	Orlando, FL
Madison, WI	

For more information, go to **http://www1.eere.energy.gov** and select the "Solar Energy Technologies" link.

27

WE CAN ECOBUILD AMERICA

Described as an event for architects, contractors, facility managers, planners, developers, engineers, government officials, homebuilders, building and construction product manufacturers, and anyone else interested in the fascinating juncture where "ecology meets technology," the annual Ecobuild America conference is one-stop shopping for those interested in emerging sustainable technologies and trends in the renewable energy sector as they pertain to building development and construction. The event offers a variety of workshops, seminars, and lectures on all things green. For more information, go to **www.EcobuildAmerica.com.**

FACE IT

- If you're planning to build a new home, take full advantage of passive solar by orienting the length of the building along an east-west axis. Place large windows on the south or southeast wall for maximum solar gain, and limit windows on the north- and west-facing walls.

28

LIGHT ON THE WALLET

Making the commitment to install a solar system in your home is not just a commitment to renewable energy, it's also a financial commitment with long-term benefits, including the fact that a PV array will increase the value of any home by approximately half the cost of the system in place.

Nonetheless, if money is tight and you still want to make the switch to solar, your timing in looking for a loan should be good and, with time, will get better. If you live in California, you are already ahead of the game, and if you happen to be a resident of Berkeley, you are among the very lucky: in September 2008, the Berkeley City Council unanimously approved an innovative new program that provides city-backed loans to homeowners for the purpose of installing PV systems. The loans, which average $22,000, are payable over 20 years and are attached to homeowners' property tax bills. Other cities have taken note of Berkeley's plan; while Berkeley's program is funded by bonds, Palm Desert, for example, is paying for a similar program with monies from its general fund.

And that's not all, California residents: the Helio Green Energy Plan is a creative alternative to financing residential solar installations. The plan allows homeowners to enjoy the benefits of solar power without having to front the costs. Each applicant is reviewed in order to determine energy needs. Helios then designs a system and installs it—no money is exchanged. The homeowner pays for the power provided by the PV panels and Helios provides free maintenance, though homeowners are required to cover any damage to the system via personal insurance. Six years after installation, the homeowner may purchase the system from Helio. Average cost? About $18,000. Kudos, California!

AND MONEY BACK

- Rebates for installing solar power systems are increasingly common, and they act as incentives to encourage consumers to build or retrofit with solar. Call your local utility to find out if you are eligible to receive a kickback on your purchase.

29

LET THE SUN SHINE IN

Here's a clever way to bring more natural light into your home: the Sun Tunnel, a tubular skylight that can be installed onto most rooftops. With a watertight circular design (which eliminates water buildup) and a leak-proof coated steel flashing that fits most roof styles, the Sun Tunnel arrives as a kit complete with detailed installation instructions. Why not just purchase a regular skylight and call it a day, you might be wondering? Here's what makes the Sun Tunnel special: its flexible tubing can be maneuvered to avoid structural obstructions in just about any roof, and the tubing consists of Sola-film, a highly reflective and long-lasting material. For more information, go to **www.bigfrogmountain.com.**

30

IT'S GETTING HOT IN HERE

If you've ever spent time in an attic, you know that they can get pretty . . . steamy. Attics trap the hot air that rises from the lower floors of a building, and if that air isn't released, the result is a hot, stuffy, for the most part inhospitable space.

That said, attic venting is important—it cools and extends the life span of the roof and roofing materials and reduces the

Now you can release all that hot air with a solar-powered attic fan installed on your roof.

load on air-conditioning systems. Venting all that stagnant air increases the circulation of fresh air through space, reducing vapor buildup generated by showering and cooking (excess moisture in an attic can lead to all kinds of problems, from rust and rot to bacteria growth and dangerous mold counts). Now, you can release all that hot air with a solar-powered attic fan installed on your roof. Called the Natural Light Solar Attic Fan, the device reduces the temperature of the attic, in turn reducing the effort put out by air-conditioning or another cooling system. The device has a venting capacity of up to 1,200 square feet and has an optional thermostat that automatically turns off the unit in colder weather. Ask your power company if your purchase of a solar attic fan qualifies for a rebate. For more information, go to **www.solaratticfans.com.**

31
SOLAR
BEAUTIFUL

Add some beauty to a window with a solar-powered glass radiometer. The first radiometer was invented by English physicist Edward Crookes in 1870. He wanted to demonstrate, via a simple physics experiment, how light can be transformed into energy through movement. The result is a basic but functional solar power plant! It works like this: when exposed to light, the four vanes (shiny on one side and black on the other) balanced on a spindle in a partial vacuum begin to revolve. The black vane heats up faster than the shiny side, repelling air molecules from its warm surface. This tiny difference in air pressure causes the vanes to rotate. The brighter the light, the faster the rotation.

Solar radiometers are available from numerous online vendors. Simply do a search for "solar radiometer" and you'll get to a source.

GET A SOLAR MAKEOVER

* The American Solar Energy Society (ASES) is an excellent resource for all things solar. Call (303) 443-3130 or go to **www.ases.org** for more information.

32 FIELD OF GREEN

Baseball. It's a true-blue American tradition. Earnest fans. Hot dogs. Solar panels. Errr . . . solar panels? Yes, it's true. Professional baseball is officially on the green bandwagon thanks to the efforts of high-profile teams across the country. Read on.

The Boston Red Sox and the National Resources Defense Council have joined forces to turn Fenway Park into a green oasis. So far, Fenway has been equipped with 28 rooftop solar hot water heating panels that will reduce the natural gas currently used by about 30 percent. The park is also looking at solar-powered trash compactors and is beefing up its recycling program and bringing organic produce to concession stands.

At Coors Field, the Colorado Rockies' LED scoreboard runs on a 46-panel solar array that generates 9.9kW of power. The Rockies purchased the array through Xcel Energy.

The San Francisco Giants, who play at AT&T Park, are treating their fans the right way: organic hot dogs and microbrew are now available in concessions. The ballpark also boasts the largest PV array in Major League Baseball. Designed by Steven Strong's

Massachusetts-based Solar Design Associates (to learn more about solar pioneer Steven Strong, see page 49) and installed by PG&E, the system is composed of 590 solar cells capable of generating enough energy to power the team's new energy-efficient scoreboard.

The San Francisco Giants installed 590 solar panels on the exterior of their stadium to power a new scoreboard.

The Cleveland Indians, which call Jacobs Field home, were the first American League team to undergo a solar retrofit at their park. The team collaborated with Green Energy Ohio to install forty-two solar panels on a pavilion building.

33

SO COOL IT'S HOT

Solar-Cool Technologies has rolled out its solar-powered cooler. If you are thinking this is just another product, then you may have to think again. The reason being, this cooler saves time, money, and the environment. The cooler works like a utilitarian multipurpose charging tool for your laptops, phones, etc. (handy when you are out camping, picnicking, or just outdoors). More exciting than the solar concept is the cooler's capacity to keep things cool or hot (depending on what role you want it to play). With the sun's mercy, it can stay at 30 degrees below or 30 degrees above the present temperature. Isn't this cool? With respect to the environment, the makers claim that each cooler being used offsets 5,000 pounds of CO_2 per annum. The cost of this utility device is $250.

COOKIN' WITH SOLAR

Ready to become a solar-powered chef? Check out *Cooking with the Sun*, by Beth Halacy and Dan Halacy. This ingenious book offers everything from instructions for building a solar oven to a recipe for Solar Stew.

DON'T USE ALL YOUR ENERGY

Let's take a minute to review some proven ways of conserving energy. Every little step is a step in the right direction. How about:

* Using compact fluorescent light bulbs.
* Turning off the lights when you leave a room.
* Purchasing Energy Star appliances when possible (they use approximately 50 percent less energy than standard, older appliances).
* Installing water-saving showerheads.
* Turning furnaces down and air-conditioning controls higher.
* Finally repairing those drip-drip-dripping taps.
* Not leaving the refrigerator door open longer than absolutely necessary.
* Learning how to "hyper-mile"—a driving technique that saves fuel and has a calming effect!
* Cooking in a microwave instead of an oven—it's faster and, thus, more energy efficient.
* Buying a front-loading washing machine, which uses less water and energy than a standard top-loader.
* Planting native grasses and plants to reduce water consumption.
* Shopping in second-hand stores, looking for used goods online (eBay, etc.).
* Refusing to use disposable drinking cups, plates, and utensils.

* Reading the excellent *It's Easy Being Green*, by Crissy Trask, for many more ideas.

A FOREST OF SHADED PARKING

Parking lots—are they known for their aesthetic appeal? Not likely. More frequently they are quickly forgotten in-between points, segues to where you need to be. Robert Noble, the CEO of Envision Solar in La Jolla, California, wants to transform how we view parking lots by turning them into showcases of solar technology. His solar "trees" are designed to accommodate two plug-in hybrid cars. The trees provide a 120-volt socket for the cars so that they do not have to depend solely on their engines to recharge.

The design of the trees is straightforward but absolutely visionary: a single trunk supports a canopy inlaid with electricity-producing PV panels. Noble, having invested a lot of time thinking about the endless acres of unshaded (read: Hot! Unpleasant! Let's get out of here now!) paved parking lots stamped out across the United States, sees opportunity in what most of us see as a necessary but ugly blot on the landscape. The opportunity? For one, shade. Imagine it! Shaded parking lots. Consider the impact of this in a place like Phoenix, in the summer, and you get the significance. And how to shade? With groves of solar trees. Noble wants to "plant" groves of solar trees in parking lots to help shade all that asphalt. The solar panels on the trees' canopies would provide electricity for the parking lot.

And, should electric cars become more common and, thus, more in need of a place to sit and recharge, the symbiotic undercurrent of Noble's idea is clear. Beyond cars, Noble wants to plant his trees at public transit hubs and install solar groves for light-rail.

"Just as a citrus grove absorbs sunlight to produce food, a Solar Grove absorbs sunlight and produces energy."

According to the company, the Envision Solar Grove can be customized to meet individualized needs for a photovoltaic-integrated parking lot solar system. The Solar Grove, the company explains, "lends itself to a variety of surroundings and terrain that could otherwise prove challenging to more standard designs."

The design of the groves is based on the concept of "bio-mimicry," Envision says, adding, "Just as a citrus grove absorbs sunlight to produce food, a Solar Grove absorbs sunlight and produces energy. The language of the analogy continues—the frame and modules of the Solar Tree become its 'canopy,' the support structure becomes the 'limbs' and 'trunk,' while the base foundation and wiring beneath the earth is known as the 'taproot.'"

Beautifully said, Envision. We're rooting for you! (Pun sort of intended.) For more information, go to **www.envisionsolar.com.**

36
HUG THOSE TREES

The Internet is a vast, seemingly unlimited source of pretty much any kind of information you could ever want. But there's a catch: How much of that information can you trust to be accurate? And how many sites truly deserve their place in the giant web-o-sphere?

Enter a site that, without question, has earned its place as one of the best on the Web for all things green: **Treehugger.com.** The creation of ceramicist Graham Hill, Treehugger consistently makes the 25 Most Popular blogs list. Given that some 100,000 blogs are born each day around the world, that's a laudable accomplishment. That Treehugger has reached this level of success in the relatively short time since its debut in 2004 speaks to the quality of its content. The site has more than 60 writers who post some 50 articles per day, and it averages about 3 million visitors each month. How to describe it? Well, you really need to visit to capture its true brilliance, but suffice it to say that Treehugger is a clearinghouse of sorts—for articles about the environment and renewable technologies and information about books, films, and any number of deep-thought possibilities. Its latest coup: partnering with the cable network Planet Green. In the roiling sea of "www" that has become the Internet, Treehugger stands out. A word of caution: it's hard to read just one post, so give yourself some time to hang out and meander.

37

THE SKINNY ON YOUR SKIN

It seems everywhere we turn we are subjected to cautionary, sometimes terrifying, stories of the effects of exposing our unprotected skin to the rays of the sun. If we were to whole-heartedly side with the anti-sun Cassandras, we would indeed come to believe that those far-away rays do nothing beneficial to our bodies, but rather wreak havoc via wrinkled, leathery skin and deadly cancer. Absolutely, we must protect ourselves from too much sun exposure. Sunscreen works, and it should be used with a vigilance akin to choosing the right wine with dinner.

Our bodies need the healing rays of the sun in order to keep us topped off with adequate levels of vitamin D.

However, emerging medical research suggests that our bodies need the healing rays of the sun in order to keep us topped off with adequate levels of vitamin D, a nutrient vital to bone health and proper immune system function. Some doctors advocate scheduling up to 15 minutes per day of lotion-free sun exposure to keep D where it needs to be. As with all things, everything in moderation. Add a little sun to your days and the remainder of the time, use a good sunscreen. For more information on this topic, I suggest you visit **www.mercola.com.**

38

A GODLY ALLIANCE

Named in honor of the visionary Apollo space program, the Apollo Alliance is a coalition of business, labor, environmental, and community leaders that actively promotes clean energy technology and policy across the United States in the hope of reducing dependence on foreign oil, cutting environmentally damaging carbon emissions, and expanding "green sector" job opportunities. The group aims to create new jobs by promoting renewable energy policy and technology and strives to "put millions of Americans to work in a new generation of well-paid green collar jobs, and make America a global leader in clean energy products and services."

Founded in 2004, the Alliance believes the wisest route to job growth in the U.S. is via the green highway and that by extending convincing arguments for investing in clean energy technology, leaders in all sectors of business and government will respond favorably to an innovative approach to economic growth: one based on the concepts of clean energy. The group's New Energy for America report—an economic analysis of its Ten-Point Plan, which documents how the tax credits and investments it proposes would create more than 3 million new high-wage jobs in manufacturing, construction, transportation, high-tech and the public sector—is available for review at no cost at **www.apolloalliance.org.**

SUNNY STATES

Home Power magazine (required reading if you are serious about solar) has compiled a list of the 10 best states for solar energy. How did they decide who made the list? "Strong incentives, forward-thinking regulatory policies, and aggressive renewable energy goals are a good start. But what really gets the *Home Power* crew excited is any state that takes serious steps from a fossil fuel–based economy to a solar-based one."

Some of the winners might surprise you. Drum roll, please...

California; average statewide daily peak sun-hours: 5.6
Colorado; sun-hours: 5.8
Connecticut; sun-hours: 4.4
Maryland; sun-hours: 4.6
Massachusetts; sun-hours: 4.6
Minnesota; sun-hours: 4.5
New Jersey; sun-hours: 4.6
New Mexico; sun-hours: 6.2
Oregon; sun-hours: 4.4
Pennsylvania; sun-hours: 4.3

40

BLOW THAT HOT AIR

Canadian solar engineering firm Solarwall has developed a heating and ventilation system that looks like traditional metal cladding but doubles as a heater. A Solarwall system costs about the same as construction of a metal wall but provides free heating and ventilation for the life of the building. The Solarwall is an unglazed solar collector that uses perforated sheet metal to preheat ventilation air. Savings depend on geographical location, but are generally in the range of $2 to $8 per square foot per year. For more information, visit **www.solarwall.com.**

POWER UP!

One of the most innovative solar products now on the market, Power Film has a variety of uses that place it firmly in the top spot of renewable energy technology. Just thirteen inches wide and up to 2,400 feet long, the rolled-up panels are constructed with a flexible yet durable polyamide substrate, which provides a paper-thin and lightweight panel as thin as 0.025 millimeters. The absorber layer is amorphous silicon, and the amount of silicon used is as low as 1 percent of the amount used in traditional panels.

The maker of Power Film has a long list of the material's potential applications; they include metal roofing, where it is conformable to a variety of architectural styles; membrane roofing, for use on commercial buildings, schools, hospitals, and warehouses; and architectural fabric, such as canopies, covered walkways, sports stadiums, airports, and convention centers. For more information, go to **www.powerfilmsolar.com.**

COOL SHADES FOR WINDOWS

For a relatively inexpensive way to cool the interiors of your home, reduce glare, and protect your furniture and carpeting from fading, consider covering your windows with sheets of window-tinting material. *Real Goods* offers affordable tinting kits for a variety of window sizes and claims its tinting film reduces UV transmission by 97 percent and decreases heat penetration inside the home by 60 percent. The material can be applied easily to wet windows or Plexiglas, and it is held in place by static electricity, not adhesive. What happens when the season shifts and you want to invite that warming heat into your home? It's simple: just peel off the material and let the sun shine in.

Other types of window tinting kits are available online. Just do a search for "window tint kit" and you should find plenty of options.

THIS ROOF'S ON FIRE

One of the most compelling advances in solar technology is the solar shingle, which looks like an ordinary roof shingle but is composed of thin-film PV cells. Despite their next-to-nothing profile, amorphous silicon shingles are powerful harnessers of the sun's energy. In addition, they tend to be more powerful than regular solar panels due to their ramped-up efficiency and ability to absorb more sunlight than other solar options on the market. Their thinness does not equate with flimsiness, either: the reality is that solar shingles are sturdy and long lasting and as such are a wise investment.

In most cases, solar shingles require an under-decking of ventilated plywood to mitigate the great quantities of heat they absorb. They also protect the house itself: when positioned in the same overlapping fashion as regular shingles, they protect the roof from the sun and other effects from the weather.

The silicon shingles are powerful harnessers of the sun's energy, and tend to be more powerful than regular solar panels due to their ability to absorb more sunlight than other solar options on the market.

The shingles' wiring is threaded through the roof deck and connected to the solar inverter. They are impervious to shifting thanks to the heavy-duty heat-activated glue used to attach them to the roof. Estimates reveal that the shingles pay for themselves over their average 20-year life span.

Besides providing solar power in an efficient, low-profile manner, the shingles can be the perfect solution in neighborhoods where regular PV panels might be met with resistance. Solar panel shingles blend easily with other roof materials, making them practically invisible from a distance.

44
GLOW-IN-THE-SUN PAINT

If research and development continues as planned, the latest product in the solar technology arsenal should be available soon. Inexpensive PV paint has been invented in the United Kingdom in a joint venture between researchers at Swansea University and the steel industry and is pushing its way toward production and commercial availability. Imagine the possibilities! The paint, composed of dye and electrolytes that can be applied as a paste to sheets of steel, has the potential to change how buildings integrate solar power systems into their inner workings. Four layers of paint are applied to each sheet of metal. When light hits the solar cells, the molecules within release electrons into an electron collector and circuit. Then, the electrons move back into the dye.

Solar paint has some advantages over PV panels. For one, it can absorb light across the visible spectrum, which means that production of solar-generated electricity would not stop or be hindered on cloudy days. And for that we wish the developers nothing but success!

45

RIDING TOWARD THE LIGHT

Now this is really something to smile about: a solar-powered motorized bicycle. The invention of an innovative and eco-minded man named Peter Sandler, the E-V Sunny "photo-optic" bike can be had for a cool $1,795. Developed in Canada, the E-V Sunny boasts PV panels that transform it from a run-of-the-mill two-wheeler to an altogether novel form of transportation.

This bike is not for racing, though: with its all-aluminum frame, sun-powered motor, and battery, it weighs in at about 44 pounds. The bike's front hub motor is fully encased and waterproof and rated to 350 watts. Speeds of up to 18 miles per hour are possible with the bike's power-assist feature.

For now the bikes are a special-order specialty item, but let's hope we see more of them on the road, and soon. Fortunately, the E-V Sunny has a top-quality saddle seat with "comfort sus-pension"—because even greenies like a little cush on the tush.

For more information go to **www.therapyproducts.com.**

46
MORE FLEXIBLE THAN A GYMNAST

The solar energy sector is aiming to make the technology as versatile and user-friendly as possible. To that end, rigid solar panels have morphed into flexible versions that are easy to use, lightweight, and transportable, making them ideal in a variety of situations, such as when a portable power system is needed. No longer relegated to a fixed-in-place existence, flexible solar panels can be folded or rolled up and easily stowed for hiking, camping, and travel.

Flexible solar panels are manufactured in a process called thin-film deposition, which applies thin layers of superconducting silicon onto a substrate that can be flexed, folded, and bent. Putting a flexible solar panel to work involves little more than unrolling it and placing it in a sunny location. The use options are abundant and include charging mobile phones and laptops, as well as marine and RV batteries.

LIGHT YEARS AHEAD: AL GORE

No book about the environment would be complete without a mention of Al Gore, the man who seems to have already lived many lifetimes in one. The former vice president appears to have moved seamlessly from the world of politics to assume the title of environmental guru.

A full list of Gore's accomplishments would take considerably more space than these pages can offer, but a summary is warranted. Let's start with his winning the 2007 Nobel Peace Prize, an event that provided him with a world stage on which to reiterate his years-long warning about global warming, that it is "the greatest challenge we've ever faced." He went on to say, "We face a true planetary emergency. The climate crisis is not a political issue, it is a moral and spiritual challenge to all of humanity."

> ## "The climate crisis is not a political issue, it is a moral and spiritual challenge to all of humanity."

When Gore's documentary film, *An Inconvenient Truth*, won two Oscars, it became evident without question that the world was paying attention to his words of caution and finding solace in his hopeful vision for fixing what is wrong.

A prolific writer, Gore has authored numerous articles and books, including *The Assault on Reason, An Inconvenient Truth* (in both book and DVD format), *Earth in the Balance*, and *Joined at the Heart*.

Gore continues to devote his time to a variety of projects, including The Alliance for Climate Protection, The Climate Project, Live Earth, An Inconvenient Truth, and Generation Investment Management. To learn more about this dynamic environmental leader, go to **www.algore.com**.

BAN THE HUMVEE—
GET A SUNVEE!

If you want to wow the neighbors and make a statement about renewable energy, take a look at the SunVee.

SunVee stands for "solar utility neighborhood vehicle." It features solar panels integrated into the body, which charge batteries that in turn power an electric motor. Billed as a "practical vehicle for trips with passengers and cargo," the SunVee has a range of about 30 miles and a top speed of 25 miles per hour.

The SunVee concept is the work of Kelly Hart, who designed and built his first solar vehicle in 1999—the Sunmobile, powered both by solar energy and pedaling.

See for yourself: **www.sunvee.com**.

CUP OF SOLAR BREW

Did you know that:

* In the United States alone, some 400 million cups of coffee are consumed every day? No surprise, then, that the U.S. is the world's leading coffee consumer.
* Coffee accounts for 75 percent of all the caffeine consumed in the United States.
* Every year, more than 100 million bags of coffee make their way to market.

In a word, WOW. So we like our coffee. And, if you are reading this book, you are likely an eco-conscious consumer who looks for ways to support businesses that don't place profits over the health of the planet.

Enter brothers Dave and Mike Hartkop, purveyors of fine coffee. Why are they different from any other coffee roaster? Because they roast their beans using the power of the sun.

Dave and Mike are the founders of Solar Roast Coffee (www.solarroast.com), which began in Oregon and now operates out of sunny Pueblo, Colorado. They roast their coffee in a marvelous device of their own invention: the Helios 4 solar concentrator, an upgraded and more powerful model of the original roaster that can roast 30 pounds of coffee in as little as 15–25 minutes. The roaster features a large mirror array situated on a motorized rotating platform, which allows the unit to follow the sun across its arc in the sky, from its rising in the east to its setting in the west. That's not all this sophisticated roaster can do: it is also equipped with a winch system that can tip the entire array up (like a large easel, the brothers explain) to follow the path of the sun vertically as it rises and sets. Solar panels power the motors. On cloudy days, a conventionally powered back-up heat source allows business to proceed uninterrupted. The Helios 4 is a far cry from the brothers' initial design: an old satellite dish covered with plastic mirrors.

Solar Roast Coffee offers retail and wholesale purchasing options. For ordering information, call (719) 544-3515 or browse the Hartkop's entertaining website, where you can also order a compostable traveler's coffee mug made from plastic derived from corn plants.

SEARCHING FOR BRIGHT IDEAS

Located in Golden, Colorado, and Washington, D.C., the National Renewable Energy Laboratory (NREL) is the primary research center and lab for renewable energy and energy-efficient research and development in the United States. The lab began operating in 1977 as the Solar Energy Research Institute. In 1991 it was designated a national laboratory of the U.S. Department of Energy (DOE) and its name was changed to NREL. The lab aims to advance the energy goals of the DOE's Office of Energy Efficiency and Renewable Energy and beyond, guiding renewable energy goals from research and development to the commercial marketplace.

Solar technology is a key area of R&D at the lab. Its Solar

Energy Technologies Program performs research in two major areas of renewables: photovoltaics and solar thermal. The lab's PV work involves research into PV-related materials, the development of PV cells in several material systems, and working with the PV industry to speed up the manufacturing capacity and market availability of PV technologies.

Regarding solar thermal, the lab is working with the solar industry to lower the cost of solar water-heating systems through the creation and testing of new polymer materials and is developing parabolic trough technology (a reliable power source for large-scale utility plants) for solar electricity generation. Although trough technology is not yet financially feasible in today's energy market, the lab aims to reduce costs associated with the technology so that it can become a viable component of the nation's energy equation.

A visitor center is located at the Golden site and can be reached at (303) 384-6565. For information on job opportunities, call the public affairs office at (303) 275-4090. And, to learn more about the lab's many areas of research and development, go to **www.nrel.gov.**

POOL POWER

If you own a swimming pool, you already know it takes plenty of cash to keep the water clean and warm. Reduce your eco-footprint by replacing your grid-connected heating and cleaning system with a solar-powered alternative. AAA Solar of New Mexico has a system that will keep your pool fresh and comfortable for about $1,075–$2,490, fully installed.

52

BY THE LIGHT OF THE
{SOLAR-POWERED} LANTERN

The lovely Isabella catalog (**www.IsabellaCatalog.com**) features beautiful Chinese-inspired lanterns that can be strung up in trees and around patios—and which are powered by the sun. This means no wires or plugs to contend with (and disrupt the eye-soothing scene). When placed for maximum sun exposure, the lanterns soak up sunshine and, when the light fades, automatically light up.

Constructed of weather-resistant, silk-like nylon, the lanterns are available (as of this writing) in square and teardrop shapes and are a very reasonable price of $24.95. When fully charged with the included AAA rechargeable battery, they provide 6–8 hours of dreamy, ethereal light. Whoever created these must be a nice person.

53

LIGHT UP THE RADIO

Gama Sonic's portable solar lamp with built-in AM/FM radio solves two issues at once: the need for light and the need for music and news. The lamp is useful in the outdoors (camping, sailing, anywhere an outlet is not available) and features an upper torch for reading. It comes with an AC/DC adapter that will charge the rechargeable battery at home at night, and its solar panel can be adjusted for maximum sun exposure.

Gama Sonic also manufactures solar-charged lights for sheds, garages, greenhouses, and boat houses; solar accent lights and spotlights for eco-friendly landscaping; an ingenious solar-powered address light that makes it possible to see the street number in the dark (the device charges by day and automatically turns on at night); a solar-powered flashlight with key chain that charges in just 30 minutes; and a patio umbrella constructed with LED lights embedded into its inner upper poles. The umbrella's solar panel sits discreetly atop the canopy, omitting the need for extra wiring. It uses a rechargeable battery to hold the day's solar reserves. For more information go to www.gamasonic.com.

54 SUN-POWERED PRIUS

The Toyota Prius, the hybrid vehicle that has become a symbol of environmental enlightenment and is the most fuel-efficient car sold in the United States, just got even better. The redesigned third-generation 2010 Prius has an average fuel economy of 50 mpg and can reach 60 miles per hour faster than earlier models. But it's the latest feature—a tilt-and-slide moonroof embedded with solar panels capable of generating enough power to run the air conditioner on hot days—that has enviro-types wagging their tongues all the way to car dealers nationwide.

With its decision to give consumers the option of the Kyocera solar cells on its high-end version of the car, now the world's most popular hybrid, Toyota became the first major automaker to integrate solar technology into a vehicle.

Says the company: "When the vehicle is parked in direct sunlight, these solar panels power a fan that brings in outside air, ventilating the cabin close to ambient temperature. The cool technology continues with a button on the key fob that activates that air conditioning system within 30 yards of the vehicle. The cabin will cool to the pre-set temperature level, without turning on the engine."

For more information on the 2010 Prius, go to **www.toyota.com.**

SOLAR INNOVATOR: ANSON FOGEL

Who: *Owner and CEO of Carbondale, Colorado–based Inpower Systems, which provides retail solar power setups and green energy consulting.*

TMO: Do most people know what they want when they walk through your doors?
FOGEL: Usually not, so we are careful to go through all the necessary steps to educate them and also determine what they truly need to reduce their fuel and electricity consumption. We discuss economics. If someone is looking to make a new house solar [versus a retrofit], we work on how to make that building as energy efficient as possible from the start.

TMO: What is one of the biggest concerns clients express regarding solar?
FOGEL: Aesthetics. It has to look good. Americans tend to buy with their hearts and egos, so if you can make it fun and cool and visually pleasing, then people can relate to it on an emotional level, and they'll invest in it.

TMO: Tell us about the PowerView software you developed. What does it do?

FOGEL: It tracks, in real time, how much energy a client's house is using or creating at any given moment. Clients love to be that closely connected to their energy habits. (For more information on PowerView, see #56, page 90.)

SUNNY TV 56

One of the greatest joys of investing in solar energy goes beyond the thrill of knowing that you are doing your bit for the planet. It comes when you can actually see how your investment is paying off, day by day, hour by hour.

Purveyors of PV panels understand the enormity of that thrill, and as such increasing numbers of them are working to offer their customers the ability to watch their PV cells in action.

Customers can log on to an individual account and watch their solar systems operate in real time.

One such company is Colorado-based InPower Systems (see #55, page 89), which has developed its own monitoring software called PowerView. PowerView makes it possible for customers to log on to an individual account and watch their solar systems operate in real time; they can track carbon saved, energy produced, and energy bought and sold.

PowerView, says company founder Anson Fogel, also serves as the clients' automatic connection to InPower Systems' service department. In other words, let's say your PVs don't seem to be operating at full potential. Maybe they're a little down in the dumps, you reason. PowerView takes the mystery out of the equation, says Fogel, adding, "If your solar system has any problem at any time, we'll dispatch a service technician to fix it within 48 hours—we're usually aware of any issues before you are."

PowerView is included in the price of some of the solar packages InPower sells, and upgrades can be purchased if desired. Check out the live demo at **www.inpowersystems.com.**

57

A SUNSHINY DAY OF EVENTS

Solar Power International: **www.solarpowerconference.com**

Ecobuild America: Sustainable, Green and High-Performance Solutions for the Built Environment: **www.EcobuildAmerica.com**

Green Business Conference: **www.coopamerica.biz**

Greenbuild International Conference & Expo: **www.greenbuildexpo.org**

WORD TO THE WISE

- This you need to know: some state rebate programs actually penalize consumers who install their own solar energy systems rather than hire a licensed contractor to do the work. Make sure you know the exact requirements of your state's rebate/incentive program before you begin.

NOW FOR A LITTLE LIGHT POETRY

Learning to Praise Again

With brusque scent of warmed sagebrush
the longtime sun reappears in the field
and renders the tall graying grass into gold.

Exhausted, I sought what was missing.
Instead, I find what was here all along:
the rising, the rising again, the rising again

and the myth of the rising, the faithful sun
at the center. Tale of night. Unfaithful worship.
Fable of cloud and day.

Under foot, crumbling, waning, change.
Prickly pear spines where pink coral grew.
Mesas fallen and falling. Last wing. Lost map.

And the sunlight braids its long fingers
through the wind's mutinous mane

and strokes a glaze to what is here,

doesn't care if we chant or repent or pray.
Even now, even now, even now it shines
whether we're worthy or not.

—*Rosemerry Wahtola Trommer*

*Organic fruit grower and life-lover Rosemerry Wahtola Trommer lives
near Telluride, Colorado, where she serves as poet laureate of San
Miguel County. Visit her at **www.wordwoman.com**.*

59
INVALUABLE WEBSITES

The following websites will keep you up-to-date on advances in solar technology and policy:

www.popularlogistics.com   www.metaefficient.com
www.huffingtonpost.com   www.solarbuzz.com

60
A CITY THAT'S
LIGHT YEARS AHEAD

Meet the eco-city of Freiburg, a twelfth-century town located in the southwestern part of Germany. Freiburg has a population of just 217,000, but it has become famous the world over for its dedication to renewable energy sources, particularly solar. The town has become an eco-tourist destination, thanks to such marvels as the Heliotrope, a rotating house equipped with a large rooftop solar panel that tracks the sun, absorbing its energy. Designed by solar architect Rolf Disch, Heliotrope is just one example of how Freiburg has embraced solar technology. Solar panels are seemingly everywhere in this sunny hamlet, including on the town's soccer stadium and incorporated into entire neighborhoods.

The Freiburg city council thrust the municipality into the renewable energy sector back in 1992, with a broad-sweeping resolution that revealed a strong commitment to renewable alternatives. For example, the council mandated that all new structures on city land be "low-energy"—in other words, that they focus on both active and passive solar energy.

More than a third of Freiburg's residents do not drive a car and, according to a special National Geographic report on climate change, per capital carbon dioxide emissions in the area have fallen 10 percent in the last decade.

Nonetheless, the town still has far to go: despite its heroic attempts to transition into renewable energy, less than 1 percent of its electricity comes from the sun.

61
PLANTING A NEW WAVE OF SOLAR

The country of Dubai is often in the news for its spectacular architectural development. Now, the country with no lack of sunshine is poised to enter into solar manufacturing technology with the construction of the world's largest solar panel production plant.

The Solar Technologies FZE photovoltaic production facility is expected to come online in late 2010 and will produce PV panels capable of generating 130 megawatts of power on an annual basis.

The announcement of the plant was made at the Green Dubai World Forum 2008. Plans are for a 1 million-square-foot plant at Dubai's Technopark.

62

POWER IN THE BAG

Solar power has entered the realm of haute couture. Check out the clever handbag designed by C'N'C Costume National. For a cool $1,905, you can acquire the leather and suede satchel-style tote, which features a small built-in PV panel that allows the lady on the go to charge her cell phone and iPod without having to search for an electrical outlet. As of this writing, the bag was available at Tru Grace, (914) 273-9600. Though not couture, Noon Solar's functional and subtly stylish Sawyer messenger bag is equipped with a solar panel designed to charge its lithium-ion battery, but its eco-stature doesn't stop there. The bag is made from leather and dyed hemp, and is 100 percent biodegradable. The company also offers a nice variety of other savvy designs. The Sawyer bag retails for $375. For more information about the company and its vision, go to www.noonsolar.com.

COOKING LIGHT

Don't be intimated by the thought of cooking with solar. It can be a great (and zero-cost) alternative to conventional methods. All solar cookers work in a similar way: they focus the rays of the sun into a concise area and retain the heat gain, capable of reaching up to 600 degrees. You don't have to spend a fortune to get one, either: how does $40 sound? And it can fold to a portable 13-inch square, so you can take it on your next camping trip. Of course you could spend more, but aside from aesthetics and price, any properly built solar oven can roast meats, fish, and chicken; bake cookies, cakes, and breads (yum: muffins!); steam vegetables; and boil pasta, lentils, beans, and rice to perfection.

Using the sun to cook food and pasteurize water (thus preventing waterborne diseases) has been a lifesaver in developing countries, and humanitarian organizations are working hard to provide basic solar ovens to communities across the globe, in the process vastly improving quality of life and helping to slow the devastating effects of deforestation and desertification caused by burning wood.

Here's a quick run-down of how solar ovens work their magic:

1. **Concentrating sunlight**: A mirror or reflective metal concentrates the sun's rays into a small, well-defined cooking area. One solar cooker even uses an accordion-fold reflective car sunshade to trap that potent energy. Talk about multi-tasking!

2. **Turning light into heat**: The color black is key here, as it makes the cooker work more efficiently. For example, a black pan will absorb sunlight and convert it to heat. Also, the better a pan conducts heat, the faster the oven will work, but keep in mind that solar cooking is going to be a different experience than throwing a frozen dinner into the microwave. Cooking with the sun takes longer than conventional methods, but the trade-off is that it requires less hands-on time.

3. **Retaining heat**: The cooker won't work if precious captured heat is allowed to escape. You can trap heat with either a plastic bag or a glass cover. Trapping heat is especially important on chilly, overcast days, because it will help the cooker reach its desired temperature.

Most solar ovens tap into at least two of these techniques to produce the high temperatures required for cooking. A quick Web search will put you in touch with organizations that promote solar cooking and help you locate manufacturers of a wide range of ovens, from the rustic and basic to the more refined and elegant. You can even learn to build your own solar oven. Here are a few sites to get you started: **www.solarovens.org** and **www.solarcooking.org.** Kids (and adults, too, let's be fair) will enjoy the solar cooking lesson at **www.pbskids.org/zoom/activities/sci/solarcookers.html.**

SUNNY-SIDE UP!

Many of us tried this as kids, but we could never quite get it right, ending up with a mess of uncooked or partially cooked eggs all over the road. If you want to prove your cooking-eggs-on-pavement prowess, try this method for perfect eggs. Pass the salt!

The following technique is courtesy of Gavin D.J. Harper and is featured in his wonderful book, *Solar Energy Projects for the Evil Genius: 50 Do-It-Yourself Projects.*

First you will need eggs, oil, and a hot, sunny day. Add to that a black cast-iron frying pan, a sheet of glass, and an asphalt surface.

If eggs aren't your thing, try baking a batch of cookies using the dashboard of your car!

Place the pan on the asphalt, add the oil, and cover the pan with the glass. Both the pan and the asphalt will soak up the sun's heat, and this heat will transfer to the cooking oil. Crack an egg into the pan and watch as it begins to cook immediately. Again cover the pan with the glass. The result? An evenly cooked breakfast, sunny-side up.

If eggs aren't your thing, try baking a batch of cookies using the dashboard of your car! It has been done, successfully, even. And who needs an air freshener when your olfactory cells can be treated to the aroma of fresh chocolate chip confections? Here's how to do it: place drops of cookie dough on a black baking tray. (Remember to use a black tray; other colors will derail your culinary experiment, although eating cookie dough is not a shabby alternative.) Place the tray on the dashboard of your car, make sure all the windows are rolled up, and park in a sunny spot. A few hours later, voilà! Cookies for the drive home.

65

SUNNY NEWS, FOR REAL

The Internet is a sprawling, sometimes unwieldy, informational beast. You can click your way to just about any topic and opinion on said topic, but the problem is you can't always rely on the veracity of what you find. Let's take a moment to thank the very wonderful **www.solarbuzz.com** for vetting the following solar-themed daily news sites. Solar Buzz calls itself a "portal to the world of solar energy" and the description could not be more true. So, click away! You're in good hands.

Solar Industry News from National Renewable Energy
Laboratories, National Center for Photovoltaics (USA/Global)

Solar News online from **WorldNews.com** (USA)

Green Building News by Iris Communications Inc. (USA)

News Stories about Solar: The Energie Letter, E-mail from IWR
(in German/English) (Germany)

News Stories (and archives) of Sandia National Laboratories
(USA)

Energy Publications News Service, Energy-Tech online (USA)

Solar Brief (in German, French, English) (Germany)

Green Energy News (USA)

Green Power Daily News from Green Power Network (USA)

Renewable Energy News from SolarAccess (USA)

Renewable Energy News from Caddet (the Centre for the Analysis
and Dissemination of Demonstrated Energy Technologies)
(USA)

Renewable Energy News (from **WorldsNews.com**) (USA)

Environmental News Service (from Lycos) (USA)

66

SOLAR CITY

Elon Musk, the co-founder of PayPal, has a strong interest in green technology. One of his latest ventures is SolarCity, a company committed to "providing sustainable, cost-effective solar solutions for many applications, from a single-family home to a commercial property."

SolarCity wants to make it possible for the mass market to obtain solar technology in an economically viable way. Its Solar-Lease program offers economic assistance to homeowners who want to switch to solar. Financing packages include low initial payments, which enable the consumer to benefit from solar without having to worry about high up-front costs, and a no-stress pay-as-you-go monthly lease payment plan.

SolarCity currently services the following areas:

San Francisco Bay Area, CA
San Jose, CA
Los Angeles, CA
Fresno, CA
San Diego, CA
Sacramento, CA
Portland, OR
Phoenix, AZ

For more information, go to **www.solarcity.com.**

STUDENTS OF THE SUN

Future generations of Earth's stewards are learning about solar technology thanks to the Pacific Gas and Electric Company's (PG&E) Solar Schools Program, which provides funding for grid-connected solar electricity installations designed to teach students about the benefits of renewable energy. The preferred system size is 1 kilowatt because it is both relatively inexpensive and can be installed quickly, and a small PV system can be placed for maximum visibility for students and the local neighborhood. Why the emphasis on visibility? The company explains: "This is because they [the solar panels] will remind each class of students that enters the school that part of their electricity is coming from solar energy. And because the systems will be up for years, each new generation will not know life without just a little bit of solar electricity, and we hope that that little bit goes a long way."

In addition to reducing schools' power bills by 1–2 percent, the systems are being integrated into curricula for science, math, history, and art. Each system is connected to an online data monitoring service that allows students and the community at large to observe real-time solar electricity production and witness firsthand the environmental impact of clean, renewable energy. Furthermore, students can compare the PV power of their school with other schools across the state. In northern and central California, teachers can sign up for free one-day solar energy training workshops.

Based in San Francisco, the Pacific Gas and Electric Company is one of the largest combination natural gas and electric utilities in the United States. In partnership with the Foundation for

Environmental Education, the company aims to donate a PV system to 40 K–12 public schools each year. Any K–12 public school
within the PG&E service area that is currently getting its electricity
from PG&E is eligible to apply, and schools within underserved or
rural communities will receive first priority in the selection process.

For more information, go to **http://www.pge.com/solarschools/**.

68
LIGHTEN YOUR TAXES

The collective cheer that went up the day it was announced that
federal financial incentives for solar installations had been extended was not just jubilant—it was a roar of happiness tinged
with relief and fresh hope for the future of renewable energy.

Here's what happened: in late 2008, after Congress had tried
for months to come to consensus on an extension of renewable
energy tax credits, the House of Representatives swept in and
passed the green incentive plan, attached to a broad-sweeping
financial bailout package, and the president signed it into law,
setting the stage for what some in the photovoltaics industry
have dubbed the "solar boom."

Here are the highlights of the legislation:

* Extends the 30 percent solar investment tax credit to year 2016.
* Lifts the $2,000 tax credit limit for residential solar, which
  means that homeowners are eligible for a 30-percent tax
  credit on PV systems installed after Dec. 31, 2008.
* Utility companies are now eligible for a 30-percent investment tax credit for large-scale PV installations.

69
GOOGLE YOUR WAY TO SOLAR SAVVY

The founders of RoofRay do not consider themselves "green freaks," but, as they explain, they do believe in "good steward-ship of our planet." Realists at heart, they subscribe to the idea that "the economics [of a solar installation] must make sense for meaningful success."

RoofRay's goal is to help future consumers of solar technol-ogy ascertain whether a PV system is financially sensible by assisting them in evaluating solar for their home or business. Founded in 2008 as a response to high gas prices, RoofRay plans to offer a number of services, including:

* Showing the potential solar power user how a solar array could be set up on their roof.

* Explanation of the costs involved.

* Analysis of what others have done in their area.

* How to use their RoofRay "solar modeling" calculator, which allows users to drag and drop a tool to figure out slope, power potential, peak, and PV panel orientation.

The service uses Google Maps to locate the property in question. The user is also asked to enter an average monthly utility bill total, current electricity usage, and bills for an entire year to tally across-the-board savings.

For more information, go to **www.roofray.com.**

70

SHOW SOME DSIRE

No, we didn't accidentally leave out a letter in that header!
DSIRE is short for Database of State Incentives for Renewable
Energy. The DSIRE website, located at **www.dsireusa.org,** is a
wealth of information on renewable energy incentives and regulatory policies administered by federal and state agencies and
local organizations. Information is provided for each state, and
the site's homepage features a U.S. map for quick access to
individual states' policies and incentives. This is one-stop brows-
ing if you want to find out if your state offers rebates for renewable energy installations and net metering, for example, and
exactly which types of technologies are eligible (photovoltaics,
wind energy, insulation, etc.). The site also offers a glossary of
incentives; links to other renewable energy resources on the
Web; a library of renewable energy policy reports, papers and
presentations involving DSIRE; and new listings and updates to
current policies. By tracking information on state, utility, local,
and selected federal incentives that promote the use of renewable energy technologies, DSIRE is able to keep current on
financial incentives for end-users who invest in renewables;
those incentives include tax credits and deductions, grants,
rebates, low-interest loans and bond programs. In addition, the
site gives detailed information on the rules, regulations, and
policies that affect the renewable technology sector.

71

GARDENING BRILLIANCE

If, like me, you yearn to grow a lush, abundant garden but live in a locale with a short growing season, help is on the way thanks to a brilliant book by New England "solar" gardeners Leandre Poisson and Gretchen Vogel Poisson titled *Solar Gardening*.

The advice and instructions inside are clear and concise if you've got a bit of the do-it-yourself in you and are comfortable following directions (or you know someone who is; I often summon my structural engineer husband for tasks like this). In summary, the book explains how to harness the growing power of direct sunlight even during the coldest months of the year and also how to protect young plants from becoming scorched during the summer, with the end result a gardener's dream: a year-round crop of organic veggies. Even small gardens, the authors claim, can yield a generous bounty across the calendar year. And all of this can be accomplished "off the grid" because properly focused sunshine replaces the need for energy derived from fossil fuels.

Whatever the season, the Poissons posit, plants will be equally happy in deadly heat and freezing cold when protected by Sun Pods and Sun Cones—simple but infinitely clever solar "appliances" designed by the authors. (The cones were inspired by the bell-shaped glass cloches that have been used by French gardeners since the days of Louis XIV.) The shape of the cones facilitates an atmosphere of optimal heat and moisture for seedlings and young plants and protects them from insects, hungry animals, and humidity-sapping wind.

LET IT ALL HANG OUT

Laundry, that everyday household chore we all love to avoid, consumes lots of energy. The good news is that washing machines that feature the U.S. Department of Energy's "Energy Guide" label, which provides specific information about how much energy, measured in kilowatt hours (kWh), the unit in question consumes, do indeed reduce energy consumption.

**Wash your clothes in your
environmentally friendly washing machine
and then tap into limitless
solar power by hanging them
on an outside line to dry.**

You've likely also seen appliances with an Energy Star rating. Energy Star, a joint program of the Environmental Protection Agency and the Department of Energy, notifies consumers of the most energy-efficient and eco-friendly appliances on the market. On average, according to the DOE, washing machines with the Energy Star designation use up to 50 percent less energy than their non-labeled peers.

So far so good, right? Well, not exactly. As washing machines have made significant advances in their energy efficiency prowess, clothes dryers have fallen behind the eco-wagon. The unfortunate reality is that, as of this writing, there is no require-ment that dryers display the Energy Guide label, which makes comparing the efficiency (or non-efficiency) of different models difficult. And, as the astute folks over at the *Real Goods Solar Living Source Book* point out, "Manufacturers [of clothes dryers] have little incentive to improve efficiency."

Harrumph! But there is a way around this discrepancy. Wash your clothes in your environmentally friendly washing machine and then tap into limitless solar power by hanging them on an outside line to dry. Alternately, you can hang them on a rack in-doors, in a room with plenty of natural light.

If drying your clothes and linens outdoors is not an option and you don't have enough indoor space for the task, there are ways to increase the efficiency of your dryer. One of the most important things you can do is clean the lint filter after each use; allowing it to become clogged will reduce airflow in the machine and increase drying time (and can be a safety hazard, to boot). Also, wait until you have a full load to begin drying and, if you have more than one load to dry, dry each one back to back to soak up the machine's residual heat. Finally, check the outdoor exhaust vent: is it clear and clean? Make sure the flapper is not stuck or hindered from opening and closing.

SAN FRAN SOLAR

Nice job, San Francisco! In June 2008, Mayor Gavin Newsom signed into law an innovative new solar incentive program to encourage more PV installations. The city and county of San Francisco will now offer incentives to residents and businesses that install PV systems on their own properties. The program, called GoSolarSF, combined with federal tax credits and the California Solar Initiative, could pay for up to half the cost or more of a PV system installed within the city's boundaries. GoSolarSF provides incentives ranging from $3,000 to $6,000 for residents and up to $10,000 for businesses, and low-income residents can qualify for $5,000.

SUNNY MYTHS AND LEGENDS

Myth: Electricity generated by solar power cannot serve any significant portion of the electricity needs of the United States or the world.
Fact: PV technology can meet electricity demand at any scale. To illustrate: the solar energy potential in a 100-square-mile area of Nevada could supply the United States with all its electricity (about 800 gigawatts) using only modestly efficient commercial PV modules.

Myth: Solar energy can solve all of our needs and do everything—at this exact point in time.
Fact: While solar energy is on its way toward becoming a major part of the world's energy portfolio, the industry can't meet all needs at this time. However, it's important now to lay the foundation by making the right investments in solar technology and manufacturing.

Myth: Solar energy cannot significantly offset environmental emissions.
Fact: PV systems produce no atmospheric emissions or greenhouse gases. In fact, when compared to fossil fuel power, each kilowatt of solar electricity annually offsets up to 16 kilograms of nitrogen oxides, 9 kilograms of sulfur oxides, and 2,300 kilograms of carbon dioxide.

Myth: The manufacture of PV is a polluting industry.
Fact: The PV world can't technically take credit for being 100 percent non-polluting, but neither is it a major environmental, safety, or health problem: As far as emissions go from manufacturing, photovoltaics are indeed "cleaner" than fossil fuel sources.

Myth: Solar is a cottage industry that appeals only to smaller niche markets.

Fact: The business of solar shows significant growth each year. The PV industry is expected to grow to a $10 billion–$15 billion per year industry by 2025.

BE IN CHARGE

What to give the gadget-loving person who has everything? Try the solar laptop charger and portable power kit by Earthtech Products. The kit includes a 25-watt "Sunlinq" foldable solar panel and the "XPower Powerpack 300 Plus," which in everyday language means that it can provide up to 300 watts of output of portable electricity and backup power—anywhere. So if you have a friend who's planning a trip to Antarctica or simply wants to get away from it all (but not completely) and needs a working laptop, this might be the perfect gift. The unit provides up to 6 hours of runtime for a 25-watt laptop. For more information, go to **www.earthtechproducts.com.**

76

COOL OFF WITH THE SUN

Here's something else for the person who has everything: a solar-powered fridge/freezer. The Steca PF 166 refrigerator/freezer runs on a single 70-watt PV module and features a fully programmable temperature control mechanism, automatic voltage detection, and fast cooling due to compressor speed control. For more information, go to **www.stecasolar.com.**

77

DIY THE SOLAR WAY

If you're looking for a fun weekend (or two) do-it-yourself solar project, consider making a solar heater for less than $500. It can be done, insists Gary Reysa of **www.builditsolar.com.** In fact, he's taken the time make this heater, proving that switching to solar can be surprisingly inexpensive. Reysa provides step-by-step instructions for the project on his website, which are found in the "DIY" section on the home page.

78

AN ALOHA STATE OF MIND

In June 2008, Hawaii governor Linda Lingle signed into law a bill that mandates the installation of solar hot water heating systems in all new single-family homes, beginning in 2010. Her reasoning for the law, the first of its kind in the United States, is solid and visionary: "This solar power legislation is another important step

The fiftieth state relies more heavily on imported fossil fuels than any other state in the nation.

in our long-term plan for energy independence in Hawaii," she told the Associated Press, which also reported that the fiftieth state relies more heavily on imported fossil fuels than any other in the nation. Indeed, state data reveals that approximately 90 percent of Hawaii's energy sources currently come from foreign countries.

In summary, the law mandates that building permits will only be issued if the construction plan includes a solar water heater system. No solar hot water heater = no permit. The rules will be lifted in areas of dense forestation and limited solar gain. Overall, state legislators and renewable energy experts anticipate the law will reduce Hawaii's energy costs by up to 30 percent. Furthermore, according to the Hawaii chapter of the Sierra Club, state leaders have set a goal of 70 percent renewable energy use by 2030.

79

GETTING TO A BOILING POINT

In addition to generating "clean and green" electricity, solar technology can be applied to generate hot water for your home. The following is a summary of an excellent discussion of solar hot water on the U.S. Department of Energy's Energy Efficiency and Renewable Energy website (**www.eere.energy.gov**).

Also called solar domestic hot water systems, solar water heaters are a cost-effective way to heat the water you use at home. These heaters can be installed and used in a wide range of climates and their fuel (sunshine) costs nothing at all!

Solar hot water heaters are fairly straightforward. They rely on the working relationship forged between storage tanks and solar collectors. Active heaters (versus their passive counterparts) are equipped with circulating pumps and controls.

You can choose between a two-tank and one-tank installation. Two-tank heating systems work this way: water is preheated in the solar heater and then moved to a conventional water heater. One-tank systems are exactly what they sound like: the solar-heated water is combined with the backup heater.

Residential heaters use a variety of solar collectors, including:

* Flat-Plate Collector: An insulated, weatherproof box that contains a dark absorber plate placed under a glass or plastic cover.
* Integral Collector-Storage Systems: Also called "batch" systems, they have one or more black tanks or tubes in an insulated, glazed box. Unheated water passes through the solar collector and retains that heat gain. The heated water is then sent to the backup heater, where it is stored.
* Evacuated-tube solar collectors: These are installed as parallel rows of transparent glass tubes. Each tube features a glass outer tube and a metal absorber tube attached to something called a "fin," which absorbs solar radiation and prevents heat loss. This type of collector is more commonly used in commercial applications.

To learn (a lot) more, go to the EERE website and search for "solar hot water." There you'll find a wealth of information on solar hot water systems.

SOLAR DEGREES

The ad for San Juan College's renewable energy degree program posits a compelling question: "As the sun sets on the age of fossil fuels, where does your future lie?"

The future is indeed bright for those who take their interest in clean energy a step further with a college degree.

Located in sunny Farmington, New Mexico, San Juan College offers a program designed to give students a solid foundation in the fundamental design and installation techniques required to work with renewable technologies. The concentration in photovoltaic system design and installation is offered as an A.A.S. degree or a one-year certificate. The difference between the degree and the certificate is that although both share the same courses, the certificate is for students who already have a degree or who work in a related industry. The degree includes general education courses added to the core content. The program focuses on PV system design and installation, and introduces students to the concepts of wind, micro-hydro, and fuel-cell technology.

For more information about the program and the application process, go to **www.sanjuancollege.edu.**

CAVEAT EMPTOR: SOLAR BEWARE

Make sure you know what you're buying when you decide to install a solar hot water system. The Solar Rating and Certification Corporation (SRCC) provides a certification and rating program for solar hot water collectors, as well as solar water and swimming pool heating systems. For more information, go to **www.solar-rating.org.**

CHECK OUT THESE WHEELS

Evan Tilley, a high school student in Ridgway, a small town in southwestern Colorado a stone's throw from the famous Telluride ski resort, is not the kind of kid who sits around playing video games for fun or watches endless hours of television. Tilley, a soft-spoken young man with a thoughtful, introspective manner, is not willing to let his brain go numb with meaningless activity. Instead, this future creator of computer-generated animation spends his downtime poring over the myriad details of an award-winning solar-powered car, the work of Tilley and the three other solar whiz-kids (Cole McKenzie, Aaron Daughtry, and Stephanie Hanshaw) who comprise the Sunshine Mountain Traveler "Steel Demon" team.

Tilley is the captain of the team, which is led by advisor and sponsor Tom Johnson, who provides the teens with ideas but is not allowed to work on the car. The impetus behind the development of a solar car was to learn the intricacies of solar cells and additional necessary components, such as batteries. The team's car has participated in a variety of races, including one at the Texas Motor Speedway (where it placed fourth out of an international roster of more advanced cars) and the cross-country Dallas-to-Denver excursion, an event that tests both the car and the driver for endurance and creativity should problems arise on the road.

The most important thing is that this three-wheel, scrappy-looking car runs— and it runs the tail off some of the hipper, better-funded designs on the track.

The car travels along at a nice clip of about 10–15 miles per hour. And, to be honest, it doesn't look like much. Parts of it feature that universal holder-together, duct tape. It looks, well, unwieldy. And heavy, very heavy. In fact, it weighs just 1,300 pounds. But the most important thing is that this three-wheel, scrappy-looking car runs—and it runs the tail off some of the hipper, better-funded designs on the track.

Tilley explains that funding is minimal—it's up to the team to raise the cash to keep the car going. [At this writing, the team was up for a potentially significant donation, which would allow for needed improvements to the Steel Demon.] Money goes into materials; for example, a new steering rod and better alignment and suspension tools. The car was built for about $12,000—a rare feat, given that most cars on the winning level cost many times this much. The most expensive components? Batteries, Tilley says.

Tilley's involvement with the team was the result of his strong science background and fascination with the technology that makes a car run on sunshine. Are you inspired to build your own solar-powered vehicle? Tilley offers five tips to help make the job easier:

* Make the car lightweight, otherwise you get too much of what Tilley calls "bad friction"—friction that will cause the car to drag and pull its alignment out of whack.
* Always have an up-to-date wiring diagram on hand in case you need to make a quick fix on the road.
* Take into consideration the weight of the driver: a heavier driver will move the wheels out of alignment, which in turn will create bad friction. Take the time to adjust the alignment each time a new driver sits in the driver's seat. [Tilley's team is currently fundraising to purchase a higher-end alignment system that won't shift.]
* Remember your sprockets! More sprocket teeth can give you a higher speed but will sometimes give you . . . wait for it . . . bad friction. Sometimes fewer sprocket teeth can increase efficiency.
* And finally, keep at it. Says Tilley: "You will have a lot of problems at all times." The message is clear: don't give up. The construction of a solar car should be viewed as a process, not a singular task.

83

SUN, SUN, SUN YOUR BOAT

Want to teach your kids about solar technology? Log on to **www.instructables.com** and search for "solar boat." There you'll find detailed instructions for making a toy boat powered by sunshine, as well as many other fun and educational solar projects. Kids are the future; let's work together to get them excited about renewable energy!

FLY THE SOLAR SKIES

Is it a bird? A plane? Well, yes, it's a plane, but what kind of plane? A solar-powered plane? Yes, it's true. Believe!

The Solar Impulse, an ambitious project led by aviation innovators Bertrand Piccard and Andre Borschberg, is now in development and is scheduled to take to the skies for test flights in 2009. The solar-powered aircraft has been designed to promote renewable energy technology and energy efficiency. The creators of the Solar Impulse plan to fly it around the world sans fuel or polluting emissions. The goal is to circumnavigate the globe in 2011, propelled solely by solar energy.

More than an example of extreme technology, the Solar Impulse is meant to be a solar ambassador, spreading the message of the possibilities of renewable energy and getting people excited by the idea of something so unusual finding its wings with rays of sunlight. To learn more, go to **www.solarimpulse.com.**

LIGHTEN UP!

Even solar energy aficionados need to take a break and play a little every now and then. Solar toys are the perfect way to unwind, and you can find numerous kinds, with varying skill levels, at **www.explore4fun.com.** Take a look. Feel the need for a long-lasting flower to place on your office or kitchen windowsill? Then the solar-powered sunflower is made for you. Or, how about a sundial, a solar UFO, a photon solar racecar, or a "sunprint" kit? All can be found on this whimsical website. Take some time and get silly. Saving the planet should be FUN!

FESTIVAL OF BRIGHT IDEAS

Every Memorial Day weekend, the small town of Telluride, Colorado, awakens from its post-ski season downtime to host the annual Mountainfilm Festival, which is, by all accounts, much more than a film festival. In the three decades since its debut, the event has continued to attract bigger and bigger crowds, and along with that its mission has evolved into a multi-faceted strategic goal. In summary, the festival aims to educate and inspire its audience about issues pertaining to a wide range of noteworthy subjects, including conservation/environmental issues/renewable energy (solar, wind, etc.), worldwide culture, mountaineering and other forms of time-honored outdoor exploration, government/policy and, even, the thrill (for some) of shooting down the side of a mountain armed only with two narrow slats composed of high-tech materials beneath one's feet (those would be skis). The eclectic folks who fly, drive, bus, bike, and hitchhike to this former mining town (now A+ ski resort) that sits bumped up against the sheer walls of a formidable box canyon arrive each year ready and eager to learn about how to protect and preserve our precious environment, open up new avenues of understanding between the West and other cultures, and regain a sense of wonderment in the natural world. For more information, go to **www.mountainfilm.org.**

SOLAR APPEAL

Good news for the 2008 Solar Power International convention and trade show held in San Diego, California: a record 20,000 people (20 percent of whom were from outside the United States) showed up to learn about the latest and greatest in the rapidly advancing arena of solar technology. Sponsored by the Solar Electric Power Association and the Solar Energy Industries Association, the convention has grown from 60 exhibitors in 2003 to 425 in 2008. The 2009 event will accommodate some 800 exhibitors.

SOLAR . . . CEMETERIES?

Talk about unusually innovative! The town of Santa Coloma de Gramenet, near Barcelona, recently installed 462 grid-tied solar panels atop the mausoleums in its cemetery. And why did they do this, you might be thinking? Seems the town was eager to embrace solar technology but couldn't find any unoccupied land

In a moment of life-changing *ah ha!*, the creative and scientific minds behind the project turned their attention to the town's cemetery—it sits on flat, open land and gets plenty of sun. It was, in all respects, the perfect place.

that met the main criteria of a successful solar array: open and flat, and with excellent year-round sun exposure. In fact, Santa Coloma is so packed that its 124,000 residents barely manage to squeeze themselves into the one-and-a-half-square-mile city boundary. In a moment of life-changing *ah ha!,* the creative and scientific minds behind the project turned their attention to the town's cemetery—it sits on flat, open land and gets plenty of sun. It was, in all respects, the perfect place. Well, except for the fact that it is a cemetery.

It was not a popular plan at first. Opponents worried that a solar array would disrespect the peaceful resting place of the deceased. In response, town hall and cemetery officials embarked on a widespread public relations campaign to convince wary folks that the project was worthy of such placement, and that it would be installed and maintained with tender, loving care and, most of all, respect for those who had left this world.

The solar panels, which sit atop the mausoleums, face due south and produce as much energy as the annual consumption of 60 single-family homes. The electricity feeds into the local power grid and is expected to prevent some 62 tons of carbon dioxide from entering the atmosphere.

Says Esteve Serret, director of Conste-Live Energy, the renewable energy company that runs the solar cemetery, "The best tribute we can pay to our ancestors, whatever your religion may be, is to generate clean energy for new generations. That is our leitmotif."

89
LIGHTING THE PATH

In 2008, *U.S. News and World Report* named Amory Lovins, co-founder of the Rocky Mountain Institute, one of "America's Best Leaders." The honor is apropos for a man who, as the magazine points out, " . . . has been arguing—in journals, at conferences, to big-name CEOs and Pentagon officials, and, for that matter, anyone who will listen—that the inefficient use of natural resources is one of the main culprits behind the country's energy problems."

But Lovins is not necessarily all about building a brigade of happy "green" people. He approaches the quest for renewable sources of energy like a businessman views the bottom line: if it's not economically feasible and satisfying, it's not going to capture the minds and hearts of those being asked to make the break from fossil fuels. Show people they can make money with renewables, Lovins posits, and they will more likely stand up and take notice.

The Colorado-based Rocky Mountain Institute has headquarters in Snowmass and another office in downtown Boulder. RMI calls itself a "think and do" tank, and its founder is something of an eccentric, a big-brained scientist trained as a physicist at Harvard and Oxford who then went on to follow his passion of making renewable energy and energy efficiency key solutions to global warming, or, as he puts it, "global weirding." Long an advocate for solar-generated electricity, the bane of his existence is that so much of the empty roof space in this country is not put toward an eco-conscious use when those acres and acres of surface could be used to support PV panels.

RMI is an independent, entrepreneurial, nonprofit organization, and it aims for its work to have a "strong emphasis on market-based solutions." For more information, go to **www.rmi.org.** Be sure to check out the online tour of the headquarters facility, which features everything from a solar hot water system to a fully functioning greenhouse with pond.

90

CHARGE IT WITH SOLAR

The folks at *Real Goods* have done it again by offering a gadget that, once learned about, becomes one of those must-have devices. Their Universal Solar Charger is, the company says, the "lightest, fastest solar charger on the market." This handy unit delivers a straight charge to portable electronics lacking in juice: iPod, Blackberry, and cell phone (Nokia, Samsung, Sony, Ericsson, Siemens, or Motorola). It's easy to use, too: just unfold it, connect the mini USB cord with the proper adapter tip, and your device will be fully charged in two to three hours of direct sunlight. For more information, go to **www.realgoods.com** and search for "Universal Solar Charger."

91

GET ACTIVE!

My hope is that you are ready to take direct action to encourage your local and/or state government to make serious steps toward a solar-powered future. Activism is all fine and dandy, but where to start? Here are some ways to begin volunteering for the planet:

* Start a renewable energy "support group" at which you and others concerned about the nation's current dependence on

fossil fuels can brainstorm strategies for reaching the people who can make a difference.

* The Solar Energy Industries Association (SEIA) needs your support if you are or plan to become a professional working in the field of renewables. Make it a point to participate in SEIA events at state and regional levels. To learn more about SEIA, go to **www.seia.org.**

* Write a letter to your state representative expressing your views about solar energy and what you would like to see happen in your state.

* Learn as much as you can. Read books. Surf the Internet. Talk to professionals about what they envision for the future.

* Make your green vote count; at times you might have to cross party lines to vote for the candidate who has the best interests of the planet at heart.

* Offer to be a clearinghouse of sorts for people who want to know about renewable energy. Share the information you have gathered (of course respecting copyrights, but some information, including that posted on the U.S. Department of Energy website, for example, is free to the public).

* Hold a solar fund-raiser. Donate the money to an eco-minded organization in your area, or choose a national nonprofit and send them a check.

* Write opinion letters to your local newspaper, or volunteer to write a column about the environment, if you have the time and feel comfortable putting your writing out there for public scrutiny. If you don't yet feel comfortable publishing your writing, ask a writer-friend to help you organize your thoughts.

92

MAKING RAISINS IN THE SUN

The health benefits of a diet rich in whole foods, versus their processed counterparts, are increasingly evident. Sometimes, however, the hectic pace of modern life can make it difficult to find nutrient-filled snacks and the tendency is to grab whatever might be available at the time (we shudder to think!).

Dried fruits and vegetables fit the bill as worthy snacks, and having them around is a wise idea. And, because this is a book about solar energy, guess what: some very bright and innovative folks determined to be hands-on with their food have engineered special dehydrators that operate on nothing but good old-fashioned sunshine.

A detailed explanation (along with photos) of solar food dehydrators is available at **www.geopathfinder.com** (click on the "Food Preservation" link on the left-side menu). I recommend you take the time to read through the fascinating explanation of and instructions for this tummy-friendly technology. Building a solar dehydrator would be a perfect weekend project for teaching kids about the benefits of renewable energy and also to give them an intimate look at how food is produced (no, it doesn't always come in plastic packages with zip-tight fasteners).

The website lists the basics of a solar dehydrator:

* Glazing (glass or greenhouse plastics);
* Black surface over the food (metal or fabric);
* Food-safe screen to hold food;
* Corrugated, galvanized metal roofing tilted toward the sun.

Here's how it works: sunlight goes through the clear glazing and hits the black surface, heating it. This heat then radiates from the black surface to the food screen below. The sloped metal roofing on which everything rests reflects heat back up toward the food, and its corrugations act as crucial airspace

135

beneath the screen for allowing "bad" humid air to escape via natural convection.

For even more in-depth reading, check out *A Pantry Full of Sunshine* by Larisa Walk, who, with partner Robert A. Dahse, owns and operates the Geopathfinder website. This book and others are available for purchase on the site. By the way, it's obvious that Walk and Dahse know their stuff: they have lived off the grid for more than 25 years, and they grow all of their own food.

SUN BATHING

I'd like to tell you a personal story now. Some time ago, during my adventurous twenties, I traveled to the Everest region of Nepal to volunteer at a high-altitude treatment clinic that served trekkers, mountaineers on their way to scale the highest peak on the planet, and those who helped get them there: the Sherpas and the porters. The clinic was . . . well, let's just say it was *rustic*. Light came from candles, heat from several creaky, barely working kerosene lanterns. The act of getting warm water was an hours-long process. To begin with, you had to carry it in from a nearby river in a heavy, tarnished metal pot. Then that pot had to sit above a meager flame until, a long while later, little bubbles began to announce the presence of something divine and sublime: water about to boil.

There was no shower, and everyone in the clinic wore extra layers of fleece to disguise their body odor. (I didn't say this story would be pretty.) On sunny days, those intrepid enough to withstand freezing temperatures in the name of being clean (I

I can recall, clearly, how it felt to take my first solar shower in the Nepali Khumbu, at the base of Everest, a mountain so tall it forms its own jet stream. I had not properly bathed in what seemed like a month. I had washcloth-bathed, yes, but I craved the feel of warm water sliding down my tired, altitude-weary body.

wasn't one of them) would allow themselves to be doused with water from a nearby creek as they scrubbed with eco-friendly soap, frantically, hurried, as in, "What I am thinking, doing this?" They turned slightly blue all right—but they were *clean*.

Then something downright celebratory happened. A generous soul gifted a solar shower to the clinic. It was easy to use: Fill it with water upon rising early in the morning and hang it outside in full sun until the water in its black bag heated up. Its design was simple and yet clever: a heavy-duty vinyl bag, a hook to support the bag, and a dangling hose with a shower-head terminus for gentle and even water flow. Bliss.

I can recall, clearly, how it felt to take my first solar shower in the Nepali Khumbu, at the base of Everest, a mountain so tall it forms its own jet stream. I had not properly bathed in what seemed like a month. I had washcloth-bathed, yes, but I craved the feel of warm water sliding down my tired, altitude-weary body. I remember the giddy anticipation of stepping under the black bag, my privacy secured by a makeshift shower stall consisting of two ancient pieces of sheet metal propped up against each other, and releasing the spigot, allowing the water to flow.

And it was hot! So hot, so good. I quickly washed my waist-length hair, unwound it from its tight braid, thrilled to the goosebumps on my skin as a breeze kicked up.

And then, this wonderful adventure turned into Hell. A vicious "100-year blizzard," as the locals call them, swept through the region, burying people and livestock and destroying entire villages with a series of unrelenting avalanches that roared down the mountainsides like freight trains. Go back to November 1995, if you like, and Google it. Trekkers, climbers, porters, Sherpas, local villagers—all stumbled into the tiny stone clinic, desperate for medicine, a helicopter ride to the relative sanity of the city, a cure, however unrealistic, for feet, hands, eyeballs, even knees frostbitten beyond repair. The trekking paths lay buried beneath four feet of snow, heavy as cement, the only passage narrow, tunnel-like intrusions created by brave locals and the yaks that had managed to survive. It turned dark in that corner of the world, and the solar shower was put away. People were dying. There was work to do. But the memories of my time there, some good but most of them sad, angry, and still unresolved, do include the few times I bathed in water warmed by the golden Himalayan sun. And as I get older and wiser (gulp!), I now see that this is the way of life: The sublime moments line up next to the somber times, the days of abundance give way to restriction and closure.

So, dear readers, thank you for indulging me. All of this was my way of saying: Go buy an outdoor solar shower. Don't wait to go camping or trekking or fishing or mountain biking or boating or cross country skiing to use it. Hang it up in your yard, even, let the sun work its infinite magic, and feel just how close you are to nature, to the Earth.

94

A LITTLE LIGHT READING

These magazines and journals are excellent sources of information about renewable energy. *Mother Earth News*, *Home Power*, *Dwell*, *Popular Science*, *National Geographic*, *Fast Company*, *E: The Environmental Magazine*, *Solar Today* (publication of the American Solar Energy Society).

95

ENLIGHTENING BOOKS

Bookstores and online book retailers such as Amazon and Barnes and Noble provide plenty of options for consumers seeking information on renewable energy solutions, sustainability, and green living. In order to help you navigate the offerings, I've done some of the legwork for you. Here are a few of my favorites, in no particular order:

The Complete Idiot's Guide to Solar Power for your Home,
   by Dan Ramsey with David Hughes (Alpha, a member of the
   Penguin Group (USA), Inc., second edition, 2007).
*The Solar Electric House: Energy for the Environmentally Responsive
   Energy-Independent Home,* by Steven J. Strong and William G.
   Scheller (Sustainability Press, 1994).

The Solar House: Passive Heating and Cooling, by Daniel D. Chiras (Chelsea Green Publishing Company, 2002).

It's Easy Being Green, by Crissy Trask (Gibbs Smith, Publisher, 2006).

Go Green: How to Build an Earth-Friendly Community, by Nancy H. Taylor (Gibbs Smith, Publisher, 2008).

Green Living: The E Magazine Handbook for Living Lightly on the Earth, by the editors of E/The Environmental Magazine (Plume, published by the Penguin Group, 2005).

Solar Energy Projects for the Evil Genius: 50 Build-It-Yourself Projects, by Gavin D.J. Harper (McGraw-Hill, 2007).

Sunracing, by Richard and Melissa King (Human Resource Development Press, 1993).

Cooking with the Sun, by Beth Halacy (Morning Sun Press, 1992).

Solar Cooking for Home and Camp, by Linda Frederick Yaffe (Stackpole Books, 2007).

Cradle to Cradle: Remaking the Way We Make Things, by William McDonough and Michael Braungart (North Point Press, a division of Farrar, Straus and Giroux, 2002).

The Passive Solar House, by James Kachadorian (Chelsea Green Publishing Company, 2006).

A Golden Thread: 2,500 Years of Solar Architecture and Technology, by Ken Butti and John Perlin (Cheshire Books, 1980).

The Easy Guide to Solar Electric, by Adi Pieper (ADI Solar, 2007).

Eco-Women: Protectors of the Earth, by Willow Ann Sirch (Fulcrum Publishing, 2009).

96

SOLID STIRLING

"Creating a brighter future for humanity through solar energy."

That's the stated goal of Stirling Energy Systems. The company has developed what it calls the SunCatcher, a 25-kW solar power system that tracks the sun and focuses solar energy onto a powerful conversion unit. This in turn converts the heat to "grid-quality electricity."

The SunCatcher combines a mirrored concentrator dish with a high-efficiency Stirling engine specially designed to convert sunlight to electricity. What's most compelling about SunCatchers is that they DO NOT employ photovoltaics. SES states that PV technology is not yet "abundant enough or cost-effective enough to meet any large-scale demands."

The SunCatcher solar dish is similar in shape to a large satellite (approximately 38 inches in diameter) and clad in curved mirrors. The dishes are programmed to face the sun and focus that energy on a collector. The collector is in turn connected to a Stirling engine, which takes that thermal power and uses it to heat hydrogen in a closed-loop system. From there, expanding hydrogen gas forms a pressure wave on the pistons of the engine, which spins an electric motor, generating electricity with no fuel cost or pollution. "This technology is referred to as solar thermal or concentrating solar power," the company explains.

The current market for the SunCatcher is utility-scale power generation versus small-scale residential or commercial use.

As of this writing, SES was in the process of developing two solar sites in California. Referred to as Solar 1 and Solar 2, these two phases are "significant first steps in deploying large-scale renewable solar technology as a commercial energy project. When fully completed, both sites will have a combined generating capacity of 1,750 MW," the company says. Imagine: thousands of SunCatchers doing their part to feed electricity to the grid.

To learn more about this amazingly innovative company, go to **www.stirlingenergy.com.**

97 SUNSHINE IN A BOTTLE

The waterproof, frosted glass "Sun Jar" by Tobias Wong captures sunshine and stores it for use at night. Each jar contains a small solar power cell and a rechargeable battery to provide about 5 hours of grid-free light. The soft glow that emits from the jar rivals any candlelight for peaceful, cozy ambiance. Available at **www.inhabit.com, www.charlesandmarie.com,** and other Internet retailers. Retail price: $44.

IN PRAISE OF FRESH AIR

Is the interior of your car feeling a little stuffy these days? Are you not keen to leave your windows rolled down—even a smidge—to allow fresh air in while you are away from your vehicle? Not to worry: Earthtech Products makes a solar-powered automobile vent, aptly named the AutoVent SPV, that runs on solar energy and keeps that closed-in environment fresh and free of hot, stale air, humidity, and pet odors. Installation is quick and easy: attach the included weatherproof strips to the ventilator, then place it on top of the window edge and close the window. The unit exchanges the air every 20 minutes. At this writing, the gadget was on sale for $29.99—which is inexpensive enough to give it a try. Could this become a favorite stocking stuffer?

99

A BOOK YOU SHOULD READ

Am I actually advising you, dear reader, to purchase a book other than mine? Yes, I am. Very much so. And here's why: *The 30th Anniversary Real Goods Solar Living Source Book* is a true marvel. Edited by John Schaeffer and published by Gaiam Real Goods, the 634-page tome is thankfully in paperback, otherwise it might be too heavy to lift. Here's what *Real Goods* has to say about its masterpiece: "(It) is the ultimate resource on renewable energy, sustainable living, alternative construction, green building, homesteading, off-the-grid living and alternative transportation."

I'm happy to recommend it. It's a nice bookend to *Turn Me On*. Consider the former a fresh, light appetizer. Then comes *Real Goods*—a hearty meal filled with every nutrient you'd ever want.

100

IT ALL COMES DOWN TO 1: YOU

This book is essentially a list of 100 ways to get excited about solar power. Coming up with this list was no small task. With solar technology gaining momentum at what seems like break-neck speed, finding the right balance of information to present within these pages was a challenge.

And then I arrived at #100. What could I say to end this book, how would I wrap up the information contained in items 1–99? The solution came to me easily: of course, I must celebrate the reader!

Without folks like you, those who are willing to dip their toes into the ever deepening and widening pool that is solar technology, the future would not look nearly as bright.

Without folks like you, those who are willing to dip their toes into the ever deepening and widening pool that is solar technology, the future would not look nearly as bright. True change comes from a shift in mass thinking. The only way we can save our planet is by encouraging each and every person to somehow care about saving our planet. We do not have to become experts on this sweeping topic. We do not have to necessarily understand exactly how sunlight can be channeled to power our toasters and coffeemakers. What we DO need is a collective passion for change. We desperately need a new way of thinking about how we consume our natural resources and how we can mitigate the effects of a too-long dependence on fossil fuels.

Each morning, the sun is there to greet us as we rise to meet the day. Will that sun solve every last problem we've ever considered? No. But that sun holds endless possibilities, and that you have taken the time to understand the basics of those possibilities is an accomplishment you should be proud of.

And so I say, thank you, #100, the reader who decided to care.

INDEX

ORGANIZATIONS, BUSINESSES, PRODUCTS

NOTES

NOTES

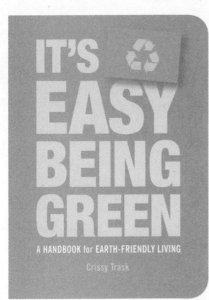